W9-BLX-249

The *Promise*
of
Buber

The Promise of Theology

Martin E. Marty, General Editor

The Promise of Buber

of

Buber

Desultory Philippics and
Irenic Affirmations

by
LOWELL D. STREIKER

J. B. LIPPINCOTT COMPANY
Philadelphia and New York

Copyright © 1969 by Lowell D. Streiker

All rights reserved

Second Printing

Printed in the United States of America

Library of Congress Catalog Card No.: 69-16963

B
3213.
B84
S7

To my beloved grandparents
Meyer and Julia Peller

200498

Foreword

Martin Buber is certainly the best-known Jewish philosopher-theologian of the twentieth century. Bearded, patriarchal, aged—as we picture him—he is gone now. Therefore a new generation includes many who feel that he must be disposed of, neglected, forgotten. It might more reasonably be contended, as Professor Streiker makes clear in the following pages, that the new generation has not only not yet exhausted the depths of Buber: it has not begun to catch up with him.

Buber's vision of interpersonality and relationship still belongs to the future, so far as an era of war and alienation (like our own) is concerned.

For his profound grasp of Jewish tradition, his biblical insight, his impact on Christianity and humanism, his coinages (like *I-Thou*), his life on "the narrow ridge," he is remembered. If some dismiss him because they see him as an existentialist and they are in the process of dismissing existentialism, they will overlook the thought of a man who is full of promise for their personal lives and theological endeavors. Streiker provides some clues to the uses of Buber and some handles on his achievements.

MARTIN E. MARTY
The University of Chicago

Contents

I

Martin E. Buber

Introduction

At the very heart of Hippiedom, in San Francisco's notorious Haight-Ashbury district, a coffee house bore the name "I-Thou." In this way the thinker most opposed to the replacing of concrete realities with labels and catchwords found his most profound work reduced to a slogan, "I-Thou," and that slogan emblazoned on a commercial establishment.

This use of Buber's characterization of the fundamental relationship of man as man is an indication of the ubiquity of his influence. Buber is inescapable, one of those thinkers who has the distinction of being "in the air." As the advocate of "dialogue"—a term which has been overused and abused nearly to death—and as the proponent of an attitude toward interpersonal relations which is memorialized by the San Francisco coffee house, he is known even to those who have read not a single line of his writings. We have grown so accustomed to the main categories of Buber's thought, e.g., the opposition of *I-Thou* or dialogic life to *I-It* manipulation, that we have condensed into a formula a man who fought all of his life against the simplistic jargon, the meaningless trivialities, which masquerade as answers to life's most basic dilemmas. But perhaps the final irony will be that the spirit of Martin Buber will elude our efforts to snare him in a net woven of his own concepts and catchwords. It may be that he will yet escape the bibliographies, footnotes, and archives to which we have consigned him. For there is something so real, so human, so compelling about this poetic prophet that it is unlikely that he would be content with the repose which we have offered him in our tributes, passing references, and scholarly recollections.

Martin Buber is remembered by many names. "Philosopher of dialogue," "Jewish existentialist," "utopian socialist," "religious reformer," "mystic," "theological anthropologist" (and "anthropological theologian"), "man of peace," "translator"—all of these designations are apt. Yet none discloses Martin Buber the man—the concrete, real, unique, unrepeatable teacher, brother, and partner.

Martin Buber was the most radical religious thinker of his age. Compared to him the Robinsons, Coxes, Dewarts, Altizers, Rubensteins, and even the Tillichs, Niebuhrs, and Barths are all tepid moderates. The dangers which Buber accepted, the difficult "narrow ridge" between extremes upon which he walked, the audacity with which he faced and accepted the paradox of man's greatness and his depravity demonstrate an unexcelled creativity and courage. When contrasted with Buber, the most revolutionary of the current crop of journalistically accredited religious rebels appear spiritual "Uncle Toms" at best.

The record of his accomplishments seems more like the achievements of a generation of gifted sages and brilliant scholars than the fruits of one lifetime. Even many of those who neglect him admit that he has been the most influential religious thinker of the twentieth century. Contemporary theology in all its guises honors him for *I and Thou,* his classic account of the primary human relationships, and for his rediscovery of Hasidism, that strange and fascinating form of Jewish piety.

But more than what Martin Buber *did* is what he *was.* What attracts the present writer—who will henceforth refer to himself in the first person, since only an "I" can enter into dialogue with the reality of another human life—is the man who contended with himself, his fellow man, his world, and his God for eighty-seven portentous years. I witness him doing "his own thing" with a courage, perseverance, and daring that I cannot help but envy. Thinkers are a dime a dozen; theologians somewhat cheaper. For all too often my generation has discovered that no real man exists behind the slogans, pronouncements, moral exhortations, and organizational handouts. More and more we are coming to realize that when someone takes it upon himself to advise others about life-and-death issues, he exposes himself to refutation *ad hominem*. Objectivity be damned. When you take it upon yourself to guide and shape another man's relation to his fellows and his God, you had better set your own house in order.

No matter how cynical they may appear, today's younger generation—the Now Generation—is a frantic lot of hero-seekers. But having witnessed the results of previous hero-worshiping, they know all too well that giants often wear their garments long in order to conceal stilts. They want challenges that try their manhood, not assurances of comfort and success. Those who offer them parades to join and bandwagons to ride misunderstand them. They are seeking their own maturity, not new fathers.

Images of the struggles, gains, and setbacks of coming to responsible adulthood flood my mind as I approach the life and thought of Martin Buber. Although maturation is a lifelong development rather than a sudden passage from childhood to adult responsibilities, I have consciously focused upon Buber's relevance to those most obviously wrestling with impending independent selfhood, i.e., the young. Coming to maturity is a process of self-realization. If I may press the beautiful ambiguity of the verb, "to realize" means both "to become aware" and "to make real." Maturity or self-realization requires that I become aware of the unique, irreplaceable potentialities of my existence as a person and that I accept the responsibility for actualizing them. Self-realization is a painful, gradual process marked by many reversals, defeats, and disappointments. Since what I was meant to be is different from what anyone else was meant to be, no formula, maxim, generalization, or dogma can distinguish for me between the real and the apparently real. Within all the circumstances which condition my existence, I must stumble along my path, discovering and actualizing the real "I."

Since, as Buber clearly recognizes, this real "I" lives in a world of other "I's," a world made up of the institutions, values, traditions, beliefs, feelings, ideas, pains, fears, and aspirations of many selves seeking realization, my quest for self-realization cannot ignore them. For this complex of interlaced relationships forms the world in which I realize myself. My coming to maturity is a development *between* the real "I" *and* other selves *and* the complex situation in which "we"—the real "I" and the other real "I's"—find ourselves. A man cannot come to maturity by shunning the duty to live responsibly with other men. Nor can a man evade the obligation to discover his distinctive selfhood by submerging it in his interpersonal responsibilities.

Every life has its rhythms. There is a time for involvement and a time for solitude. There is a time for the "I" to go out into the world to encompass and devour the new. There is a time for returning to the lonely quiet of self-examination. The quest for the yet untried, unknown, and unimaginable is what distinguishes man from all other beings. But it is the retreat to self-searching, self-criticism, and reflection which turns his individuality into humanity.

Solitude is the womb in which personality develops. Experience and the forms by which experience is assimilated are the sperm and ovum of human conception. The self must wait to be born, must wait for identity to emerge. When life emerges, it will be hungry for the new, the exhilarating, the astounding—and able to digest it.

If the "I" remains in the haven of its gestation, afraid of the new and secure in its repose, it shrivels and dies. Only the absorption of the new, surrender to the pains and joys of human existence in the world of men, can sustain the life of the self.

Life is exposure to contradiction, error, guilt, and regret.

[14]

Its deepest lessons are taught the worst of all possible ways. Man is the only creature with potential, but this potential is found only *in, through,* and *despite* the bumbling awkwardness of human development. Children become men and women by risking regret, accepting guilt, and learning from failure. It seems that the length of infancy is increasing. The years of responsibility for one's offspring spread to include college, graduate school, specialized training, and the first years of marriage. But until the umbilical cord of cash subsidy and moral guidance is cut, infancy continues. Keep a man a child for three decades, and the possibility of his maturing into a unique, creative human being fades slowly into impossibility.

Adulthood must be thrust upon us. Society, family, and the incipient adult himself must set a limit to infancy. By eighteen years of age, family has exerted its maximum influence upon us for good and for bad. Until this time, the family has every right to impose its law, order, and discipline upon those who reside under its roof and protection. At eighteen, the roof must be removed, and with it the expectation of automatic conformity. College is an opportunity for transformation of child into adult. It is neither the foe nor the lackey of parental authority. Father, mother, culture, tradition, and religion have had their chance. If they were indifferent or incompetent, it is not the task of the educational enterprise to supply remedies. It would be well if parents realized this and accepted the hard responsibilities of authority during the first eighteen years.

At eighteen the child must get away to rebel, react, rethink. It is insane to expect the young to discover the meaning of responsible, independent selfhood while exposed to the well-intentioned interferences of home. The call of Abraham to leave family and security for the wilderness of perilous experience is a summons to every eighteen-year-old.

The rhythm of maturation from eighteen to twenty-two is one of exploration and assimilation. These are the glorious years in which identity emerges despite every effort to discover it. The most absurd self-deceptions lead mysteriously to the humility, the balance, the understanding of real manhood and womanhood. *In, through,* and *despite* immature taboo-breaking, cocky relativism, and feigned disinterest, the constant image of the self takes form. It seems mandatory that you smoke pot, lose your virginity, use four-letter words for copulation and elimination, wear beads and sandals, and insult the institutions which feed, house, educate, and protect you. Unless the postadolescent abandons himself to such transgressions now, he will be doomed to commit them and greater stupidities at ages when such things are not only unseemly but absolutely absurd. For identity and singularity are the product of experiencing life for oneself as seducer *and* seduced, victor *and* victim, sinner *and* saint, hound *and* hare—in sum as giver and doer rather than as recipient and witness.

Coming to maturity is not only a matter of having experience but of integrating experience. Without exploration—venture, experimentation, partial success coupled with continual failure—there is nothing for the self to integrate. But without the reflective, critical struggle with experience, the newly gained sense of personal identity is soon dissipated. One of the purposes of liberal education should be the presentation of paradigms by which incipient adults may construct personality out of personal experience. The teaching of history, literature, philosophy, religious studies, and other subjects which place emphasis upon wrestling with the problem of meaning are decisive. How sad it is to find Plato, the Buddha, Hesse, Napoleon, Marx, and Freud reduced to memorizable formulae rather than exhibited as actual examples of the one element most lacking from the lives of today's young adults—the integration of experience by a centered self. College students are becoming immune to facts and information. Why, then, should humanists continue to translate struggles and conflicts necessary for the discovery of personal meaning into outlined, programed data? Commitments, purposes, challenges, and goals are contagious. The student's hunger for

[16]

direction inclines him to take quite seriously all-embracing world views and philosophies of life. Education cannot funnel signficance into young minds. But it can demonstrate the indispensability of the quest for human meaning and how others have gone about it in the past. Without the meanings and values which provide a perspective from which to regard the information, education increases the inner chaos of the student's attempt to keep a grip on himself and his world.

During the college years, the young adult is testing his potential as a human being—thinker, lover, friend, adversary, competitor, co-worker. Since each relationship is a strand of the gradually spun web with which he comes to trap his own image, it is vital that there be many relationships. The development of personality requires two essential ingredients. First, experience—good, bad, and indifferent; second, patterns—adequate, partially adequate, partially inadequate, or wholly inadequate—for the assimilation of experience and the building of life. Without programs, data remain gibberish. Without experiential data, programs are useless.

The uprootedness of the offspring of our affluent society arises directly from the lack of personally significant patterns for the construction of life. The Now Generation's war with the institutional forms of American life is prompted not as much by a disavowal of the values of the government, the universities, and the churches as by frustration at attempting to discover just what values (if any) these institutions really support. The current worldwide revolt of the young is actually a negation of negation, that is, anarchy directed against formlessness, materialism, and vulgarity. It is not that the structures are oppressive as they formerly were. Rather, they are so trivial and irrelevant that they are virtually unworthy of the energy it takes to ridicule them. After all, the guerrillas who take to the streets of Paris, invade the administration buildings at Columbia, burn their draft cards in Boston Common, and petition the Pope to remove Cardinal McIntyre are a minuscule minority compared to the vast gray army of the bored, complacent, and indifferent. And why should they not be indifferent? Is constant change for the sake of change preferable to dependable but dull stability?

It is characteristic of civilizations in process of deteriorating that forms of personal salvation multiply. As a society reaches the brink of disaster, individuals find and obtain satisfaction in a variety of ways. Some solace their fears through faith in the enduring monoliths of commerce. As Thomas Merton observes, the dedication of General Electric officials makes Trappist devotion seem sand-lot! Others retreat from the self-annihilating mass amalgamations and wander the face of the earth in search of private nirvanas. Some turn to drugs; some to God; some to both drugs and God. In our own day, the rate of dissolution and the diversity of private havens are multiplying at a mind-numbing rate. The contemporary mystery cults—replete with their gods, charismatic leaders, sacred writings, and promises of salvation—supplant one another at a bewildering rate. The psychedelic sects, the Maharishi, Marshall McLuhan, the Esalen experiment, and the many other saviors which have come and gone in recent years all offered us personal repose from the barrage of conflicting demands which overload our nervous systems and leave us comatose. But each has done little more than become a new symptom of our critical condition. Who can judge the salvific power of drugs, therapy, the New Left, or the caves of Crete—when he has not yet appropriated the Beatnik discovery of Zen, the idealism of the New Frontier, or the cash value of *Games People Play*?

To the whole panoply of contemporary redemptive sects, Martin Buber proclaims a firm, unwavering "No!" Neither in the reassuring magnitude of collectivism nor in the overwhelming intoxication of private ecstasy can a man achieve his true and full humanity. Buber not only described the path to self-realization and responsible maturity; he exemplified it. Indeed, it is impossible to separate Buber the man from Buber the thinker—which must be regarded a considerable feat in itself in this day of poll-taking image-makers. Therefore, in presenting the thought and relevance of Buber, I have attempted to keep hold of a series of crises in which his life and personality developed. First, there was the struggle of Buber the young intellectual to find his identity as a man and as a Jew. Second, there was a radical reappraisal of Buber's hard-won Jewish faith under the impact of the harsh realities of everyday experience. No sooner had Buber rethought the meaning of an ancient faith in the contemporary situation than he faced the third crisis, the sinister menace to the very existence of the Jewish people which nearly consummated its diabolic intent. The fourth and final crisis, the rebirth of the Jewish state in its ancient homeland and the peril to world peace which results from the continuing hostility of Jew and Arab, festers like an ugly sore at this very moment. With these four issues in mind, I have attempted to enter into dialogue with Martin Buber and, thereby, to indicate both the meaning and enduring significance of his life and thought.

This slim volume is not intended as a critical exposition of Buber's thought. While leaving unvoiced several of my own reservations, I have attempted to represent, elucidate, and expand upon the central themes of Buber's writings. My approach is governed by the conviction that no thinker is more pertinent to the contemporary social, intellectual, and spiritual situation than Martin Buber. I have sought to explain and to extrapolate in a manner which is faithful to Buber, consonant with the purposes of this series, and, above all, germane.

What Is a Jew?

Born in Vienna, February 8, 1878, Buber was to spend the formative years of his boyhood with his paternal grandparents as the result of the dissolution of his parents' marriage. Between the ages of four and fourteen, he lived with Salomon and Adele Buber in Lemberg, Galicia (now Lvov, Ukranian Soviet Socialist Republic). The elder Buber was one of the last leaders of the *Haskalah,* a movement which sought a renaissance of Jewish culture in the coming of age of Jewish religion within the civilization of Western Europe. A landowner, grain merchant, and mine operator as well as a philologist, Salomon Buber produced critical editions of many important Jewish texts. He was widely known for his edition of the Midrashim, ancient stories about biblical characters which embody the everyday wisdom of scholars and sages of Jewish antiquity.

Young Martin was deeply influenced by his grandmother. Although it was her practical management of the family's business ventures which freed her husband for his scholarly pursuits, she found time to acquaint herself with the world of European letters. The kindness and love which she lavished on the motherless boy taught him the meaning of human concern just as his grandfather's example produced a reverence for the collective memory of the Jewish people and a passion for transmitting it to successive generations. Without Salomon and Adele Buber, the remarkable potentiality of this child might never have been actualized. Martin Buber's later efforts as a translator of Jewish texts—particularly the superb German version of the Hebrew Scriptures which he and Franz Rosenzweig produced—as well as his respect for the concrete responsibilities of life were rooted in the early years in the home of his grandparents.

Until he was ten years old, Buber received private tutoring. His subsequent years in Polish primary and secondary schools left their mark on his spirit. In his eighties he recalled how he had felt during the obligatory devotional exercises which began each day at the secular school he had attended. The few Jewish children stood silent and unmoving with eyes fixed on the floor while the other students crossed themselves and prayed. Eight years of "mutual tolerance without mutual understanding" had a more depressing effect upon him than any overt act of intolerance. Being compelled to participate in a religious act which held no significance for him raised a lifelong antipathy to all missionary activity.

But this very antipathy raised the question of his own

[20]

identity. Lacking a sound knowledge of Jewish tradition, the meaning of his "Jewishness" haunted him during his university years at Vienna, Leipzig, and Berlin. (It is significant that Buber had substituted a talk on Schiller the German dramatist for the usual biblical exposition during his Bar Mitzvah. It is also of interest to note that Buber married a German Roman Catholic, Paula Winkler. Mrs. Buber, who wrote under the *nom de plume* of George Munk, converted to her husband's faith.) In his twenties, Buber found a provisional answer in the Zionist movement. He became a leader of those Zionists who proposed a renewal of Jewish culture rather than the creation of a Jewish state.

Zionism, born of the instinct for self-preservation at a time of increasing anti-Semitism (e.g., the Dreyfus affair), sought a refuge for the world's Jews in the re-establishment of their long-disrupted national existence. Buber's active participation in the Sixth Zionist Congress in 1902 exposed him to the charismatic but erratic personality of Theodor Herzl, the prime mover in the attempt to establish an independent Jewish nation. Buber's distaste for the uncritical nationalism of the Zionists and his own unsettled questions regarding the meaning and destiny of Judaism prompted him to withdraw from all active pursuits for five years of meditative self-examination. He found himself drawn to Hasidism, a mystical offshoot of Judaism which had flourished in the isolated villages of Poland during the mid-eighteenth century. Hasidism (derived from the Hebrew *hasid* which means holy or pious one) laid stress on inward renewal and exuberant manifestations of devotion in public worship. In the joy, ecstasy, and love of the early *Hasidim* (pious ones), Buber believed that he had found the very essence of Jewish faith. He saw in Hasidism a concentration of elements which existed in traditional Judaism, but in a much more diluted form.

The attraction of Hasidism, itself a historical relic within orthodox Judaism during Buber's youth, can only be understood against the background of rabbinic or traditional Judaism. For this reason, I would like to devote the next few paragraphs to an untechnical, somewhat oversimplified sketch of the development of Judaism.

The word "Jew" is a contraction of "Judean" referring to the descendants of the inhabitants of Judah, or Judea. Judaism, the religion of the Jews, is rooted in the history and traditions of the ancient Hebrew tribes. Although the foundation of Judaism is the Hebrew Scriptures, there is much in the Bible which is not in Judaism and much in Judaism which is not biblical. At the time of the return of several thousand Judeans from exile in Babylon in the fifth century B.C., The Law of Moses (Torah) was accepted as the charter of national existence and the rule of everyday conduct. Rigid observance of this code provided the basis for a unified social, economical, political, and religious existence. The Law of Moses became the constitution of the Jewish state, creating a corporate stability which had been lacking before the exile.

From the beginning, the role of the scholarly interpreter of the Law was paramount. The ancient traditions which became the basis of Jewish life were preserved in a tongue which few spoke. Without the services of translators, interpreters, and teachers, the Torah would have been little more than a tribal relic. The development of the codal religion which we know as traditional or rabbinic Judaism rests upon the shoulders of a succession of interpreters, commentators, and devoted students who scrupulously conveyed the ancient teachings while applying them to ever new circumstances. With the destruction of the Jewish state during the first century and the dispersal of the Jews to the four corners of the world, it was the unbroken chain of interpreters which ensured the continuity of the Jewish people.

The "diaspora" or dispersion of the Jews was really a long historical process which the Roman wars only accelerated. At no time did more than a minority of the Jews reside in Palestine. Yet the religious developments of these few centuries provided a basis for Jewish identity which transcended the boundaries of Palestine during the short period of national existence and which bound the scattered Jews together after the disappearance of the center of national worship.

United by their common codal heritage, guided by those who reinterpreted and reapplied the Law under the demands of changing conditions, Judaism preserved a dispossessed people from assimilation during times of security and from despair during times of persecution. At times respected and prosperous among alien peoples, but more often subjected to social discrimination and threats to their very lives, the Jews found meaning in both adversity and prosperity through observance of the Law as interpreted by ancient sages and classical commentators.

As centuries passed, interpreting the Law gave way to interpreting previous interpretations, then to commenting on interpretations of interpretations, next to commenting on commentaries on interpretations of interpretations, and so on. The conditions forced upon the exiles in their segregated villages or ghettos and the strictures of the Law became confused. Since there is constant interaction between even the most rigidly separated social groups, the customs and superstitions of their neighbors were unconsciously blended together to form a Jewish life style. As the modern era dawned, it became impossible to detect whether a given mode of behavior or manner of dress was prescribed by the Law or adopted from the Poles, Germans, or Russians.

As the lines of authority stretched further and further from their origin in the national existence of the ancestors of the Jews, a narrow obscurantism, a bookish intellectualism, tended to obstruct the vital religious forces within the Jewish communities. The spread of democratic ideals in the aftermath of the French Revolution and the Napoleonic wars, as well as migration to the New World, removed the external compulsions which had given the Jew little choice but to adhere to the traditions and mores of his community. Previously a Jew had no choice but to be a Jew. But now as a citizen of Germany or Poland or France or Great Britain or the United States, he was no more automatically a Jew than his Gentile neighbors were automatically Christians. To be sure, he was still a nominal Jew as they were nominal Christians. But the options which were open to the Christian to be whatever sort of Christian he chose to be were now open to the Jew as well.

Traditional or rabbinic Judaism became a right-wing guerrilla movement which sniped away at all attempts to come to grips with the new situation. It held the allegiance of the rural villagers while losing the emerging class of artisans, merchants, professional men, and civil servants.

When it is impossible to be anything but a Jew, the Jew has no problem discovering the meaning and often tragic dimensions of his existence. Anti-Semitism has always been the surest definer of Jewishness. But when it is possible to decide for oneself what it means to be a Jew, the problem is enormous. One thing is certain. No matter how the Jew interprets his Jewishness, traditional Judaism will play a role in his self-understanding. If he is an irreligious Jew, it is because he rejects rabbinic religion. If he is a Reform Jew, it is some permanent value or "essence" of traditional Judaism which he seeks to enhance. If he is a Conservative, he finds himself defending some basic aspect of the Judaism of the Orthodox communities against the poorly reasoned and rash innovations of the liberal. Thus, in some way, that which religious Jews securely term "the Tradition" (with a capital "t") is present in any explanation of what it means to be a Jew. It is not surprising that a large percentage of America's non-Orthodox rabbis were reared in Orthodox homes.

Although the Hasidic faith in which Buber found his personal roots represents a personal choice of a highly private nature, Buber's search for the meaning of his own identity as a Jew is a paradigm of the inner struggle of every modern Jew—indeed of every modern man who reveres an ancient faith. Buber's solution was the virtual invention of a form of Jewish piety in which he could achieve personal satisfaction and fulfillment. Although his faith sprang from his studies of

[24]

Hasidism, it was a distinct reinterpretation of the faith of the Hasidic communities. Buber discovered an essential core or spirit of Hasidism which stood in constant tension with such tendencies as magic, superstition, and unyielding authoritarianism. According to Buber's account of Hasidic history, the simple message at the heart of Hasidism transcended the tyrannical leadership and inner dissent of the Hasidic communities just as the prophetic faith of ancient Israel surmounted the injustice and division which infected the religious, political, and social institutions of the first commonwealth. In his role as interpreter of the Hasidic heritage, Buber is not merely a chronicler of an unusual form of Judaism, but a prophetic voice calling the Hasidic community back to the purity of its essential faith and inviting traditional Judaism to reexamine itself in the light of Hasidic spirituality.

The fundamentals of Buber's personal reconstruction of Hasidism find graphic portrayal in his historical novel, *For the Sake of Heaven.* The novel, based on a dispute between two legendary Hasidic leaders at the time of the Napoleonic wars, concerns the nature of man's contribution to the redemption of the world. The Seer of Lublin and the Yehudi, founder of the congregation of Pshysha, find themselves in sharp disagreement on the use of magic to transform the armed conflict of their day into the final battle which will usher in the Messianic Age. The Seer believes that the end can be hastened by the exercise of power over evil forces, a power which attends the purity of life of those who shun the world to seek after God. The Yehudi is concerned with the "hallowing of life," the binding of one's life to God in all spheres of daily activity. Man's share in redemption, affirms the Yehudi, is his turning to God, his hallowing of the moment.

The Seer regards evil as a primal force which may be controlled through magical incantations and thereby forced to serve the purposes of God. But according to the Yehudi, evil is an element within man himself which only suffering and despair can redeem. To discover good is to encounter the

Shekinah or Glory of God in the world. But the *Shekinah* may only be met in the ambiguity of human existence, during those moments of our experience in which good and evil are indivisibly blended together. God's *Shekinah* is exiled in the world, separated from God just as the Jews are separated from their homeland. In the anguish of its despair, the *Shekinah* turns to man, beseeching him to set good free from evil by actualizing the potential for good of the concrete task at hand. In this way, the good man participates in the sufferings of exile, sharing with God in the redemptive process which hallows the tensions of life and ushers in the Kingdom.

The essence of Hasidism which Buber distilled permeated his life and work. Although the pressures of circumstance forced him to modify his interpretation of the meaning of Jewish existence, the fundamental conception remained unaltered during his long and fruitful career. According to Buber, the burden of Jewish faith, the Jew's *raison d'être*, is the task of actualizing unity or wholeness. The Hasidic sages had expressed this notion through the mythology of the separation of God and his *Shekinah*. They saw the *yihud* or reunification as a process to which man contributed through pious deeds and an inner turning to God. The religious life requires an alertness, an openness to the presence of God's Glory in all things and a cleaving to God with a singleness and intensity. Only the whole can make whole. The Oneness of God which Judaism proclaims is not the declaration of an abstract theological monotheism but a recognition of God's call to at-one-ment with himself. By uniting his usually divided purposes, man responds to the divine summons and takes his place as God's partner in the work of attaining wholeness or unity. Note how the words cluster together: harmony, unity, wholeness, single-minded, wholehearted, atonement. All declare the oneness of God and man's participation in that oneness. But consider the antonyms: dissension, conflict, tension, opposition, division, disorder, confusion, strife. By rejecting his place in the realization of the divine Oneness, man sacrifices his wholeness and forfeits his own self-realization.

According to Buber, the history of Judaism is the record of Jewish failure to respond to the divine call to partnership. Because the Jews have turned from the task of actualizing the *yihud*, they suffer exile, persecution, and inner dissension. The traditionalist's dedication to the study of ceremonial and legal minutiae has split the personal life into sacred and mundane concerns, thereby destroying the wholeness of life. The stultifying antiquarianism of Jewish orthodoxy has forced those who responded to the divine summons to leave the community and its life, and thus to disturb further the very wholeness which they sought. Deprived of the nourishing life blood of tradition, the esoteric sects have either withered away or yielded to the example of Orthodoxy. Hence, the Hasidic communities which persist at present are ultraorthodox cultural remnants whose strict observance and alien dress set them apart from mankind. Their Amishlike isolation, their refusal to cooperate with even the most Orthodox observant Jews, excludes them from the unity of the people of God.

The inner divisions of Judaism plunge the individual Jew into the internal confusions and interpersonal tensions characteristic of man's unredeemed existence. His lack of direction and purpose paralyzes his will to act. Without personal wholeness and singleness, man is at the mercy of conflicting demands, impulses, and urges. Such inner tension produces a persistent inability to decide or act, a habitual lack of orientation, which Buber regards as the essence and source of all evil. Only a turning to God with one's whole being can restore the wholeness of man and enable him to share in the redemptive process of reunification. For the very meaning of being a Jew is the acceptance of one's own life as a unique, unprecedented, never-to-be-repeated opportunity for the hallowing of life. To be a Jew is to acknowledge one's partnership with God in the work of recovering oneness—an indivisible, living wholeness which manifests itself in the unity of God with his creation, the harmony of man with his fellows, the peace which restores and heals the individual. Through such partnership, a man wholeheartedly proclaims with deeds as well as words the ancient confession, "Hear, O Israel, the Lord thy God, the Lord is One."

The Meaning of
Personal Existence

Ours is a time without intensity. Television, it would seem, has transformed all of reality into rapidly dissolving images of gray. We have become viewers of an endless tragi-comedy which grinds on routinely and tediously, only interrupted by an occasional commercial message. We watch and listen without stake, without interest, without involvement. Our attention shifts from actions before us to emotional states within us with the swirling rapidity of an all-engulfing cyclone. Reality speaks, touches, threatens, brings weal and woe. But all is indistinguishable. The television image is as real as the face of a neighbor. The injury and pain suffered by a stranger in the street grabs us with the same impact as the sights and sounds of mayhem on the evening news. The murder of a statesman before our all-seeing television eye touches us no more deeply than the cancellation of a situation comedy. (A mayoralty campaign in Houston, Texas, was lost by a contender whose paid political telecast pre-empted "I Love Lucy." Did the public's outrage at the time of the assassinations of Martin Luther King, Jr., and Robert F. Kennedy accomplish this much?)

All are data. All is true. All is entertained and, hopefully, entertains. Men, slogans, equations, opinions, works of art, beliefs, feelings, household appliances, the discomfort index, the beautiful people, the Gallup poll, the United Nations, nonmetallic zippers, Benjamin Spock, and Hugh Hefner—all are impenetrable bubbles, capsules of data. What is man? A fixed point of reference, a prefocused camera, before which these bubbles blow and collide until they burst or the wind carries them out of sight.

Who is responsible for the bubbles? Where do they come from and where do they go after they pass the point of observation? Cameras do not ask such questions. They merely watch.

Education—the accumulating, sorting, preserving, and distributing of information—is the fastest growing industry in America. If data-hawking seems a strange conception of education, a cursory examination of the vast educational establishment will demonstrate the accuracy of this generalization. From elementary school to postgraduate studies, there is a gigantic machine which encases reality, experience, and reflection in bubbles to be blown in the face of the pupil with the apparent intent of permanently blinding him.

Bubbles of data, untouched by human hand, barrage, bewilder, and inundate the student. The variety of bubbles is so overwhelming that only one response is possible. The student memorizes the constellation of bubbles at hand, discharges the burden of memory when examined, and forgets these particular data forever. Memorize, repeat, forget—this is the pattern year after meaningless year, subject after required subject. The greatest democracy in world history educates its children in a manner suggestive of an oppressive totalitarianism. (There are important differences, to be sure. Tyrannies spoon-feed values as well as facts. We dispense with everything but data. After all, the Constitution guarantees freedom from values.)

But finally the last maze of childhood has been run. The time has come to enjoy the "liberal" education promised as a reward for numb-bottomed, attentive, innocuous passivity. And suddenly there are bubbles in the air again. The university at which I teach numbers its students at over forty-three thousand, one third in the college of liberal arts. My colleagues and I are managers of a vast information factory which churns out millions of data bubbles for thousands of adept bubble handlers. The manner in which the final product of our efforts—the degree holder—is assembled on our four-year conveyor belt is obviously modeled on the creation of automobiles out of components obtained from a hundred competing suppliers. (Again, there is a decisive difference. Ford, General Motors, Chrysler, *et al.* know what they are building.)

Memorize, repeat, forget, and move on to the next subject. The normal load is five or six courses in as many subjects. Since the sum of the assigned readings is greater than the capacity of an electronic scanner, the student humbly waits to be told what he has read so that he may memorize only what he is told, recreate it for the final exam, and move on to the next capsule of data.

The capsule-makers work in almost complete isolation from one another. English literature, philosophy, geology, psychology, calculus, history, chemistry, French, religion, sociology—all are autonomous, autocephalous guilds of capsule-makers. The greatest care is taken to preserve the capsules created by each guild from becoming polluted by contact with another guild's products.

Since the student has no world-embracing perspective of his own, he finds it impossible to assimilate the data deluge. At best, he can entertain the information momentarily before him, read one or two of the several textbooks assigned for each course, swap outlines of what he has read with fellow students who have read one or two others (an enterprise which amounts to counterfeiting capsules), and yawn a lot— unless his accredited bubble dealer is watching, of course, since a detected yawn can turn an A into a C. The student consoles himself with the hope that if he holds on for awhile longer and controls the urge to spit in the institutional eye, he will receive the card which reads, "Pass Go. Collect $600 a month. If possible, do something honest for a change."

A bachelor's degree represents sixteen years of benign acceptance of a place in a machine which produces three products: more machines, machine parts, and machine tenders. Some (an unbelievably large percentage) become teaching machines, capable of channeling the bubbles but unable to make their own or discover any relationship among those which they convey. Some become proverbial cogs in machines, pencil pushing and rubber stamping life away in business, government, or educational bureaucracies. Others—wearing the shop aprons which identify them as police, clergy, physicians, psychiatrists, politicians, proficiency experts—lubricate, mend, and repair the machines.

The wondrous efficiency of a mass age utilizes every skill, talent, and human feeling. Everything is neatly encapsulated— people in apartments and apartmentlike automobiles; reality in formulae and slogans; politics in whatever noun currently attaches to the shopworn designation "new"; truth in the college outline series, the *New York Times,* and *Playboy;* morality in bourgeois platitudes; emotions in love songs; peace of mind in the therapists' jargon; God in the aphorisms of the latest theological craze.

The purity of each capsule is strictly maintained. Encapsulated neighbors never meet and are thus spared the embarrassments of neighborliness. (A garbage can blown a hundred yards disappears as if the wind had carried it to Tahiti.) Encapsulated ideas never mate to conceive insights and meanings. Encapsulated theologies are never exposed to the acid test of livability. Encapsulated ethical maxims are never required to grant anything more than security in return for inoffensiveness (which is encapsulation defined as virtue).

The encapsulated life is safe, clean, comfortable, and certain. But, alas, it lacks the one vital element—intensity. The individual must either flow along with the dull, insipid mainstream or take his chances in the faster, exciting, and dangerous currents which mass society shuns and declares out of bounds. The choice is intensity or respectability. For an age which seeks security in uniformity, moderation, and restraint must condemn all manifestations of private passion, personal exuberance, and individual ecstasy as essentially antisocial.

When the forces which agitate the depths of a man's soul are denied socially acceptable forms of expression, the individual will turn to the ever present demons which offer desperately craved satisfactions. The skin-on-skin delights of sexual intimacy, the psychotic beatitude of the psychedelic drugs, the engulfing tactile immediacy of electronically amplified music, the deliberately obnoxious activism of the New Left, and the terrifying unrestraint of the Hell's Angels—all are forms through which the angry army of the bored attains its moment of rapture by blowing its kazoo in the ear of society.

In his youth, Martin Buber blew a gentle kazoo. He turned to the most innocent and innocuous form of instant intensity—*religion*. The personal joy that coursed through his blood in rare moments of ecstatic union with God made endurable the drab sameness of the everyday. The responsibilities of mundane affairs became a ladder of ascent by which to reach the awesome and rapturous presence of the Other. The disappointing return to the mediocrity of ordinary life was tolerable only because of the expectation that the everyday would sooner or later dissolve once more to disclose the uncanny and mysterious Other.

In the late autumn of 1914 Buber came to a personal turning or conversion which separated him forever from the quest for religious intensity. As the result of a commonplace occurrence, the direction of his life was radically altered. One afternoon, after a morning of religious ecstasy, Buber was visited by a young stranger. The man found Buber his usual courteous, friendly, and open self. But the lingering glow of the morning's religious rapture blinded Buber to the despair and distress which had brought this visitor to his door. Buber was attentive, answering every question that the youth put to him. But he failed to intuit the real questions, the invisible inner impasse which the verbalized quandaries only concealed.

A short time later, Buber learned that his visitor had been killed in the war and that the youth had sought him "not for a chat but for a decision." Buber was overwhelmed with remorse for having neglected the anguish and need which had led the young man to his door. The realization broke upon him that his insensitivity was caused by his self-centered hunger for "religious experience." His life had been governed by a fundamental error. God, he sensed, does not call man to the satisfactions of heights of rapture during rare moments separated from the mundane. Overpowering intensity and awesome presence are not experiences to be sought for their own sake, but the natural accompaniment of a man's response with the fullness of his distinctive personal being to the responsibilities of everyday life. Religion is not the mystical flight to a realm transcending the everyday. Rather, it is an attitude of openness and expectancy amid the opportunities of each mortal hour. Religion is the acceptance of the possibility of dialogue, an inclining of one's heart and mind toward unconditional, spontaneous relation.

What we witness in Buber's reinterpretation of the meaning of religion is the shifting of elements in his understanding of Hasidism. The hallowing of life changes its role as an instrument leading to mystical ecstasy to a central place as the goal of human life. Previously, Buber had seen the hallowing of life as the arranging of one's duties into routine patterns of behavior to occupy the individual between flashes of religious fervor. But now he had become aware of *the inseparability of man's relationship to God and his relationship to his fellow man.* To leave behind the responsibilities of the everyday is to forsake God as well.

There are not two worlds of experience, the sacred and the profane. There is only the mundane world to which we may respond in two different ways. We may use, enjoy, manipulate, experience, analyze, and know the world. Or beyond this, we may regard the same world of the everyday as the context of our relationship to God. For to hallow life is to bind oneself to God in each act by responding completely, unaffectedly, openly with the wholeness of one's being to the concrete circumstances of one's life. Faith is not an intense feeling in the soul but an entrance into the whole of reality, a waiting for God's summons to partnership in the divine work of reunification. "Dialogue"—that much abused term—is the

[34]

word chosen by Buber to represent the attitude of expectant faith.

Instead of special acts, performed on "holy" days, for the purpose of obtaining favor from an extraordinary being, religion is a day-by-day life of dialogue. According to Buber's familiar distinction, men are capable of two basic attitudes toward reality, *I-Thou* and *I-It*. When we regard the realities which we encounter as *objects* to be understood, utilized, dominated, or controlled, the *I-It* attitude is paramount. There is nothing wrong in this attitude. Without the perspective of *I-It*, man would be unable to respond to the world in which he finds himself. To perceive, to feel, to imagine, to will, to think—all of these *I-It* relations are essential operations of our daily existence. Man cannot live without objectifying and responding to the elements of his experience.

The attitude of *I-Thou* designates a relationship between *subjects* or persons. The English translation is somewhat unfortunate, since the word "Thou" is usually reserved for prayer. In order to overcome the sanctimonious tone of "Thou," we should think of the relation of reciprocity and mutuality of person to person which Buber has in mind as "I-You." Although I live by virtue of my *I-It* objectivity, it is only when I address another being as "you" and am myself so addressed that my distinctive nature, my life as a person standing in relation to another person, is realized.

That which happens between an *I* and a *You* determines the uniqueness of a man, the never to be repeated meaning of his life. It is through the *I-You* relationship that personality emerges. As Buber declares: "Through the *Thou* a man becomes *I.*" For the *I* that exists apart from the web of interpersonal relations is a pale abstraction. It is through *I-You* relationships that my distinctive selfhood is born and lives. The more fully and genuinely I relate to the *You* whom I meet, the more determinately real I become. "All real living is meeting," the transforming of communication into communion.

The *I* of *I-You* encounter and the *I* of *I-It* experience differ fundamentally. The *I* of *I-It* is aware of itself as the subject which uses and controls the objects which it encounters. This *I* is the individual separated from and independent of the objective world. The essential self-world or subject-object split is the basis of man's life. Man discovers that he is a *self* in a *world* to which he *belongs.* All human thought, intentionality, and activity depend upon the recognition of this primal situation. But although man cannot live without *It,* that is, without appreciating the nonidentity of his selfhood and the objects which confront him, "he who lives with *It* alone is not a man."

The *I* of *I-It* is imprisoned in the solitude of inner experience. This *I* can deal with reality only indirectly, through abstractions, concepts, memories, and previously observed relationships. The flux and vitality of the real are captured in static generalizations like insects trapped in amber. The *I-It* attitude sorts and catalogues the objects of experience in accordance with previously discovered connections and categories. *I-It* conforms the present to the past in order to accumulate knowledge and organize life. Since the new, the unique, the unanticipated, and the mysterious cannot be subsumed under the generalizations derived from past observation, the *I-It* attitude must ignore or suppress them.

Man becomes aware of reality and shares its vital power neither in the security of inner subjectivity nor in the regularity of the external, objective world. Both pure subjectivity and pure objectivity are abstractions based on relations *between* man and man, man and nature, man and God. *I-It* experience takes place *within* a man; *I-You* encounter occurs *between* men. The *I-You,* or dialogic relation, is marked by immediacy, spontaneity, directness, and intensity. Regardless of what has occurred in the past, when I confront you without the protective armor of preconception, the astonishing, the inconceivable, flashes between us like static electricity. Do I know anything about you that I did not know before this moment of mutual presence or presentness? Do you know anything more about me? Certainly not. For knowledge is the conceivable, the predictable, by means of which I reduce you to objectivity or it-ness in order to use, control, and manipulate. But because of our meeting we are now more real as persons, each of us better prepared by the moment of mutuality to realize the distinctive, unique potentialities of his *I*.

The predictable, dependable knowledge of *It* points us to the fading world of the past. When we assimilate that which we encounter to that which we already know and control, the power and vitality of the here and now is transformed into a mere image. But the direct meeting of *I* and *You* glows with presence. That which happens between real persons radiates the force and life of the here and now. For only that which is present, which is at hand in a moment of lived sharing, possesses reality. And only the real can impress us with the awesome intensity which transforms stagnant self-sufficiency into creative mutual growth.

Where life touches life deeply as in a good marriage or a genuine friendship, each partner steps forward in the unique singleness of his nature, achieving an extent of personal development which otherwise remains hidden and unrealized. As a man responds to the distinct nature of the other, he discovers and reveals the uniqueness of his own humanity. Through such relationships and only through them can the healing, teaching, reforming, and redeeming of persons be accomplished in either the individual or the corporate spheres of man's life.

On the basis of the concrete moments of *I-You* meeting, there arise the words, generalizations, descriptions, and concepts which enable man to use and enjoy his world. The trustworthy patterns which he takes for granted—the language in which he communicates, the dependability of natural law, the consistency of the maxims which govern human behavior—rely on primal encounters with reality. The power of a word, an idea, a law, a rule, or a belief is its proximity to the concrete, immediate relationship of an *I* to a *You*. Meeting is real; reality is meeting. Memories, platitudes, and opinions are media through which meeting is conveyed and by which it is partially eclipsed. Such images of reality enable us to develop the customs, manners, and mores without which life would be shapeless and chaotic. But the further they move from the concrete and immediate, the more they obstruct the very vitality which they seek to preserve. Dialogue between beings who stand in a relationship of creative mutuality gives way to an *I-It* correlation between the individual subject and the objects of his experience. Spontaneous response to the other becomes deliberate use and manipulation.

No moment of man's life is purely *I-You* or *I-It*. The two attitudes are inextricably interwoven. There is the *You* that I *know* as a sum of qualities, a certain physical shape with certain features, observed patterns of behavior, habitual ways of reacting to given situations, etc. Such knowledge, which regards you as an *It* or object, gives me a secure basis upon which to build a relationship. For if you changed drastically from moment to moment, there would be no *You* for me to encounter. But my image of you is imperfect—a picture which constantly reacts with the unique, unpredictable *You* of our relationship. No matter how thoroughly I know you and myself, I can never fully know what will happen *between* us.

There is a primal distance between the experiencing subject and the objects of experience. The mystic, the psychotic, and the acid-tripper all seek to eradicate this distance and to lose the *I* among its objects. The *I-It* attitude saves the self from being dissolved into the sea of impressions, dreams, feeling-states, and experiences. By making the distance between the subject and objects of experience ever wider, *I-It* turns fact against fantasy, establishing the individuality of the observer. The *I-You* attitude bridges the distance by bringing subjects into relationship. Rather than merely separating the individual from the objects of his subjectivity, *I-You* determines the development of *individuality* into *personality*. The accentuation of distance turns subjectivity into the processing of data received from the senses. Entering into relation reveals the unique potentialities by virtue of which the *I* becomes a person rather than an individual.

There is a fundamental distinction between individuals and persons. The individual thickens the distance between himself and other selves. He objectifies both, reducing others to definable qualities which he may manipulate; and controlling all expressions of his own subjectivity in order to project a desired image. In the world of individuals, appearances, roles, and postures interact in such a way that the nature of the subjects is concealed behind their manifestations. As long as one contrives to produce a desired effect, he remains a mere object or appearance. When he responds with the wholeness of his being to another without calculating his gain or the image which he conveys, he becomes a person.

What is man? How may we define the essence of human life? There are, declares Buber, many ways to answer. We may describe man as the rational animal, or the tool-maker, or the symbol-creator, or the war-wager, or the child-rearer, or the beast-tamer. But what is that which makes man more than an extremely clever and adaptable mammal? The answer lies in the concept of person, a notion which combines two elements: potentiality and confirmation. Man is the only being with a potentiality. The essence of all other beings unfolds with a natural and automatic certainty. Acorns produce oak trees; worms ingest soil; the heavy falls and the light rises; rocks are hard; the offspring of raccoons are raccoons; birds migrate to warmer climes in colder weather. But man is without instincts or built-in directions. He may be influenced or he may refuse to be influenced; he may be objectified by others and objectify himself or he may put an end to objectification and retreat into a solitude which no one can penetrate. He may develop into a vicious, cunning predator or into a sensitive, loving person.

How then does a man discover his potentiality, the unique possibilities for personal development which he alone possesses? He can mimic the patterns of action, thought, and belief of his elders: like a beaver duplicating the dams of other beavers. Or he can assert his individuality by destroying all such norms. If he adopts the first course, he is nothing more than a well-socialized and benign animal. If he follows the second course, he is the enemy of his kind, a cancer which others will soon interdict or remove for their own protection. In either case, he is less than human. For neither in comformity nor in deformity does man discover his distinctive nature but only through the confirming presence of another person.

An animal has no need to be confirmed, says Buber, "for it is what it is unquestionably." But man longs to discover what he is through another who accepts, affirms, and confirms him. Although my distinctive selfhood is contained in the depths of my personal being, this hidden potentiality cannot be released until I find it present in my relation to the other. When I become a *presence* in the life of a person, that reality which makes a difference in the development of another human being, then and only then do I become the real, authentic, vital *I*.

Community is essential, for only in the unity of man with man can a person become aware of and actualize his unique selfhood. A true community is a living *We,* an aggregate of *I's* and *You's* bound together in a cluster of interpersonal relations by a common concern. Buber rejects, on the one hand, the irresponsible individualism which seeks self-realization in isolation from the concrete involvements of man's social existence, and, on the other hand, the collectivistic demand that all individual differences be submerged for the sake of a common goal. In the place of the anarchy of unbridled individualism and the totalitarian repressions of collectivism, Buber advocates a reformation of society into a community of communities, each of which unites men who share a common, direct relation to a living center, and who have an immediate relation to one another by virtue of this center. Buber insists that a society or "an organic commonwealth" can never be constructed by arbitrarily forming conglomerations of individuals but only by bringing "small and ever smaller communities" into active relationship.

Buber based his hopes for the restructuring of society on the experiences of Israel's experimental farming communes *(kibbutzim)*. He sadly admitted that Israel's socialistic experiment was of limited success due to dissension within the scattered communes, jealousy between communities, and a loss of original dedication as individuals rebelled against the incentive-sapping collectivism of life on the *kibbutzim*. Nevertheless, Buber maintained that the direction of "communalism" was of lasting significance. Wherever groups of men discover a living center which unites them in direct, immediate human encounter, they share a love and comradeship which overcomes the tragic isolation of individuals so characteristic of industrialized society. But what is this "living center" which forges bonds of communion in the midst or our unneighborly, indifferent, and atomistic mass age? What force can reverse the dehumanizing tide of objectification? How can men enter into relation when progress and survival depend upon the translation of human beings into ciphers—zip codes, area codes, social security numbers, the holes punched into college registration cards, file numbers for social workers, and, finally, grave registration numbers? Can any power restrain the objectifying process which folds, spindles, staples, and mutilates the soul of man?

There is, Buber declares, one relationship which can never degenerate into *I-It* objectivity. There is one *You* which by its very nature remains "you" to us and cannot become an *It*. There is one concern uniting men which can never become a basis for exclusive self-interest as have the purposes of all nations, labor unions, and religious fellowships. There is one directing aim which can never be translated into a social program, political plan, or ecclesiastical formula. This is "the Eternal Thou."

In the meeting of person with person, there are possibilities for mutual growth and personal satisfaction which other experiences lack. In such relationships as marriage and friendship it is not only a union of two individuals but also a creative mutuality which reveals potentialities otherwise unobservable. As two persons come to know one another intimately, to react to each other, and to find their true selves reflected in the other, something more than a union of their separate natures is discovered. The same is true of any real human relationship, wherever life touches life deeply in all the complexities of society. In all these relationships there is available a unique potential, disclosing itself to my imagination as I contemplate the concrete possibilities of our relation. In my response to the *You* of my life, I am drawn on to ever higher levels of mutual self-realization and satisfaction. This lure is the Eternal Thou.

In every sphere of life, at every moment of mutual presence, in each call upon us to respond responsibly with our whole being to the *You* at hand—we look beyond the particular or momentary *You* and glimpse the self-identical, ever-present *You*. Is this "Eternal Thou" God? Buber advises us to forget everything we associate with the word "God"—our theologies, dogmas, accepted beliefs, and self-made images. When we respond directly and wholeheartedly to persons in the variety of concrete encounters which fill the life of the authentic *I*, we are addressed by "the God of a moment, a moment God." Out of the multiplicity of such encounters emerges the unity of the single *You*. Even the man who abhors the name of God and declares himself an atheist is addressed by the Eternal Thou and responds when he "gives his whole being to addressing the *Thou* of his life, as a *Thou.* . . ."

What is man? What is God? According to Buber, the two questions are inseparable. Man is the creature with a potential which can be achieved only in relationship to other men and in relationship to God. At every moment, man participates in finitude and infinity, time and eternity. An unconditional voice calls him to partnership and fellowship. If man ignores this summons, his entrance into relation with men is doomed to futility. However, if he turns to the divine Speaker and ignores the society of human responsibilities, the Eternal Thou is blind to his attention.

For Buber, the notion that religion removes man from his involvements with nature and society is utterly false. Buber agrees with Kierkegaard, the father of modern religious existentialism, that the *I-You* relationship is exclusive in the meeting of man with man. When I meet you, you and you alone are the focal point of my consciousness. But the very opposite is true of the divine-human encounter. For one's relationship with God is inclusive of all other relationships; indeed there is no relationship without them. It is the "Gods" of a multiplicity of concrete, everyday encounters which coalesce in my imagination to form the image of the single, eternal *Thou.* The fullness of this God is no more present in any given encounter than the complete image of the personality of a poet is enclosed in a single poem. And yet, just as the poet is fully present in each of his poems, so God is manifest in every moment of meeting.

Life is hallowed and bound to God whenever a man broods over the structures, forms, institutions, and goals of his personal, interpersonal, and corporate life, seeking to open them to the creative spirit of *I-You* relationship. As Buber develops the basic insight of Hasidism, there is no absolute distinction between sacred and profane, the holy and the secular. Everything is waiting to be hallowed, to be brought into living mutual relationship in a community with a living effective Center. *To be a man is to share in the creation of such community.*

In our time without intensity we face the danger that the barrage of facts, data, news flashes, pop tunes, and trivia will turn our own subjectivity into one more object. More and more we are becoming creatures of the outward-oriented senses and strangers to our inner feelings. Man is not only finding that he is unable to relate to other selves. He is becoming increasingly alarmed by his own numb self-alienation, his inability to discover or relate to his inner self. Our children are experts with objective realities. But they are losing their capacity to internalize data, to compare fact with fact, to discover relationships between objects. One finds in their classroom responses and their written essays a security in the objective, an eagerness to pile up unrelated bits of "research." But what is alarming is the anxiety which seizes them when they are asked to evaluate, compare, or interpret.

The small minority of these students which recognizes the slipping away of their selfhood under the impact of the data-barrage desperately thrashes about attempting to recover an inner satisfaction and intensity. But their clamoring after excitement and novelty leads them to no real alternative, and accomplishes little other than a stiffening of the oppressive institutional controls. Thus, the excesses of our youthful revolutionaries destroy rather than enhance the freedoms which we cherish. Yet throughout the world today the pattern seems to be irresponsibility on the part of a coalition of the young and the Left, followed by a sharp rise in the power of the Right. Where the alternatives are revolutionary chaos or reactionary order, the juvenile glorification of the violation of standards or the imposition of rules to guarantee stability, the prevailing mood will be an anxious quest for form rather than reform.

Buber's concept of a theocentric communalism, his prophetic call for the development of authentic personhood rather than individualism or collectivism, and his hope that society could be restructured to foster both community and personality possess a relevance to the contemporary situation which we ignore at our peril. I must confess that I find more sense in Buber than in the ready assumptions, false dichotomies, and phony alternatives which currently dominate political, social, economic, and religious thought. How unfortunate it is that we have reduced Buber to a few romantic slogans and shelved him. *I and Thou* was intended as something more than a poetic work for a young man to give his fiancée to test her sensitivities before publishing the banns. There is a power in this slim book and the other writings in which Buber plumbs the dialogic essence of personality. There is a force at work which resists the steady dehumanization of man's life and the patterns of his existence. If it is success, or happiness, or satisfaction, or security that we seek, we will not be content with the disquieting, discomforting tensions of the dialogic life. If, however, it is the fullness of our humanity as citizens—educators, physicians, administrators, artists, working men and women—our share in the actualization of community which we seek, we would do well to accept the extended hand of Martin Buber.

The Spirit and the Forms

Buber would certainly agree with Paul Tillich that there is no such thing as a "revealed religion." For religion is the reception and distortion of revelation. Every religion is based upon an original moment of human encounter with the divine Thou. But the rituals, concepts, precepts and dogmas preserved by religious institutions are not; even though the original moment of direct meeting—the clear, undistorted presence of God—is embedded in them.

The religious man endures a constant tension. Without the forms of religious life, the dynamic power from which they spring would be lost. But these very structures obstruct the vital power to which they bear witness by confusing forms with spirit. Religious meaning is found *in, through,* and *despite* religion, as we noted earlier. If the seeker after religious reality and truth becomes disheartened by the religious contradiction of revelation, and discards the unsatisfactory manifestations in favor of the "pure essence" of his religion, he is left with neither essence nor distortion. If he relinquishes to ecclesiastical authority his freedom to protest the betrayal of the faith upon which the fellowship is grounded, he sacrifices his humanity and removes himself from the redemptive partnership which God offers only to men.

The impatient radical cuts himself off from the institution for the sake of the purity of his relationship with God. But since God has no message for him except in, through, and despite the community, he dooms himself to fight an egocentric "last stand" against revelation as well as its distortion. The desire to flee from the frustrations involved in struggling against the false gods of religion for the sake of the true God of divine-human encounter is easily understood. Even the Prophets despaired in the face of the constant incorrigibility of human religiosity and longed for the abolition of the temple and its cultus. Did not the God of Israel wage a relentless war against the ceremonies and beliefs which supplanted him in his own house? But if those who dishonor the divine name are destroyed, who will recall him? Since it is the fate of man to discredit all that he most cherishes, what man or institution can stand before the judgment of God?

Modern man faces a problem which is even more vexing than the interference of religion with that which it mediates. Again and again, as a Christian or a Jew in the Space Age he is forced to deal with one persistent question: What does the biblical God have to do with his day-by-day existence? The Bible and the religions which it has nourished describe a supernatural deity who dwells in the heavens, who revealed himself to certain men in a series of ancient incidents such as the miraculous exodus of the children of Israel from Egyptian bondage. According to the Christian Scriptures, this transcendent being visited our planet disguised as a man, was murdered, miraculously revived, and returned to his heavenly headquarters.

The difficulty is that the day in which we live witnesses no such interference with our affairs. We feel a disquieting discrepancy between our everyday way of looking at the world and the biblical interpretation. Under our critical, scientific scrutiny, the firm avowals of the Bible fade into racial mythologies, legends, prescientific curiosities, projections of wishes, and unfettered exaggerations. As much as we may long for the face-to-face communion with the personal God of biblical faith, we know better than to commit ourselves to what may turn out to be only an illusion. So many of our gods have died as we passed from childhood to maturity. Again and again, we have caught ourselves worshiping success, or love, or the socioeconomic status quo, or our own meager selves writ large. So many of the voices that we obeyed in the past have led us astray. All too often we have been damn fools rather than God's fools, inflicting pain and suffering humiliation in vain. Our memories of the blind canyons of dillusionment into which what we took to be the voice of God led in the past, offer little prospect of the trustworthiness of such a voice in the present. It would be perplexing enough if the only problem were the ambiguity of God's presence in the religious sphere. What really crucifies us as religious men is our own propensity for impersonating the divine voice and the seductive power of our mimicry. Truly, the human heart is an idol factory.

As we have noted, a man can always solve the problem of the ambiguity of religion by either getting out or blindly submitting, by abandoning the tempest-tossed ecclesiastical vessel or passively obeying orders which set a dead course at full speed for the shoals. But there remains an inner dilemma which neither alternative is able to resolve. Many of us acknowledge with sadness the impotence, irrelevance, and triviality of our religious institutions. Yet we hang in there for the sake of the central meanings and values which we discovered in childhood or adolescence—truths without which we never would have become the men and women we are today. The very institution which now bores, annoys, and frustrates us was undeniably the wellspring of grace.

Some men come to view the once significant rituals and creeds as ladders which brought them to spiritual self-sufficiency and which now must be kicked aside. The reason for the existence of religions, they assert, is to provide something to outgrow. When we were spiritual neophytes, we needed the image of an all-powerful, all-knowing God. But as religious adults we have learned that the word "God" refers to a certain dimension of our ordinary daily lives, a dimension upon which a "deeper" or "more authentic" way of life is established. By hallowing the Sabbath, they relate, we discovered that every day is sacred, that "God" is not a being who pertains to special activities such as prayer and special places such as churches or synagogues. Rather, "God" is a dimension of our dealings with one another. "God" is not an infinite being but an imaginary lure composed of our own sense of unfulfilled potential. The important thing is not whether such a being exists, but the function he performs. By luring us on to a fuller and more perfect humanity, this imaginary focus of aspirations is indispensable. To believe in God is not a matter of worshiping a supernatural deity but the affirmation of one's commitment to those values which best serve men in their quest for true manhood—truth, goodness, justice, beauty, and love. The religious notion of God is a hook upon which to hang these values. It is *not a supreme being but the supremacy of such humanitarian ideals* which is at stake.

To the present writer the greatest of Buber's accomplishments is the manner in which he dealt with the problem of the relevance of an ancient faith to the modern world. I am struck with awe and admiration by his vigorous efforts to recover a sense of man's continual meeting with God at the heart of Judaism and his exposure of the traditional (and not so traditional) forms of Jewish life to the litmus test of their compatibility with the divine-human encounter. Without deifying or rejecting tradition, he was able to demonstrate the viability of Judaism as a worthy commitment for contemporary man.

Buber regards all actual religions as instances of a natural and necessary error, "a fall of the spirit into spirituality." Every religion is based upon a direct meeting of a man or a community with the Eternal Thou. The subsequent religious institutions attempt to preserve original encounters by systematizing them into beliefs and practices. But all such forms of religious life come to obstruct and replace actual meeting. Soon scriptures, ritual, ceremonies, creeds, and hierarchical structures through which the religious encounter is routinized become ends in themselves, mediators of grace to which man owes unconditional obedience.

The claims of religious institutions split the spirit of man into two spheres: public and private spirituality. Since institutions are concerned with the conservation of tradition, they are bound to the past. Therefore, modern man in his quest for intensity or "presence" (presentness) turns to his own inner feelings or "religious experience." An egocentric preoccupation with seeking and having desired inner states results. But this concern overlooks the fact that the value of religious experience is dependent upon the whole life of the person and community in which such experience arises. Within the context of authentic life and genuine community the state of religious intensity is a spontaneous accompaniment rather than the goal of man's spiritual existence.

Neither feelings nor institutions can produce true life. Unless they are united in the unity of personal wholeness, each has the power to enslave and destroy. Submission to the authority of institutions blinds us to the concrete "here-and-now" situation of man's existence. Tradition ensures the rule of law and order which is the absolute *sine qua non* of human development. But it can never anticipate the demands of change. Hence, Orthodox Judaism has yet to come to terms with modern inventions such as electricity; Catholicism breathes uneasily in a world shaped by democratic rather than autocratic governments; and Protestantism underwrites a blend of capitalism and altruism which the modern welfare state rendered obsolete decades ago. It is hardly surprising that contemporary man regards the devotion of religion to the past as an obsolescent defender of the status quo and the enemy of social reform.

But the freedom promised by those who call man to rely on subjective feeling or "sincerity" is in fact a greater bondage than institutional control. For without the forms provided by institutions, man is at the mercy of the most capricious of all tyrants—his own feelings. The institution of marriage cannot guarantee an abiding relationship of mutual solace, tenderness, and satisfaction. But neither can the indefinite feeling of erotic fixation which passes for love in the minds of so many. The institutions generated by the American experience—the exacting balances of the branches of government, the tenuous equilibrium between individual liberties and public welfare, the painful patience which allows all voices to be heard and which refuses to consider any judgment final—these institutions cannot eternally defend us from personal greed, myopic self-interest, and glaring injustice. But without such structures the rule of sincere feelings soon becomes the law of the jungle. For when the lawful means of arbitrating conflicts and redressing inequities are ignored in favor of techniques which offer only immediate outlets for frustrations, the result is always a weakening of both social order and personal liberty.

We stand precariously perched on the narrow ridge between submission to the heritage of the past and the abandonment of our fate to the whims of the moment. According to Buber, a living center is required which can bind public order and personal dynamics in the wholeness of authentic human existence. Repression of the struggle between the elements of life destroys the possibility of growth, maturation, and progress. This tension must be creatively accepted, directed by individual men and societies toward the discovery of the meaning and goal of their existence. To Buber the conflicts of life represent a continual meeting of man with the eternal, central Thou. Amid the dilemmas of institutional insensitivity and personal instability, the spirit may yet be heard. Communion and community are actualizable despite the divisive pressures of competing groups and dissonant individuals. A viable combination of respect for tradition and constant self-criticism within traditions is possible. It is not easy to balance the demands of past and present, tradition and reformation. But God did not intend for life to be easy.

An indication of Buber's approach to this problem comes to us in his reaction to an unsettling story from the Hebrew Scriptures. In the fifteenth chapter of I Samuel we are told that King Saul was rejected by God through his prophet Samuel for his failure to kill Agag, the Amalekite chieftain.

Buber was convinced that the God whom he adored could not have ordered the brutal murder recorded in the biblical narrative. He contended that either the prophet had misinterpreted God or that the record had been altered by a later redactor who misunderstood the incident. It is apparent from Buber's discussion of this story that he regarded the Bible—together with all religious documents, rituals, creeds, and cultic ceremonies—as the reception and the distortion of original encounter with God.

It was not the monotheism, morality, or religion of Israel which represents its gift to Western civilization. According to Buber, the uniqueness of Israel consists of its unbroken dialogic relationship to God. The covenant of Sinai is more a marriage than a business contract. When, out of a full mutuality of love and trust, the people listens to the divine voice and obeys, the wholeness of its social, political, ethical, agricultural, and religious life exemplifies an authentic humanity which God intends for all peoples. The personal fulfillment of their lives reveals the glory of God and his call to fellowship to all nations of mankind. The Bible is the record of the people chosen by God to stand before him under the burden of such signal responsibility. It is a record of failures as well as successes, of betrayals of the covenant as well as acts of faithfulness unto death.

The biblical text has passed through many hands and has been altered in the interest of different theological attitudes. This process is itself a continuation of the divine-human encounter which the biblical materials preserve. For example, the antimonarchist bias of the scribes who edited the books of the kings is the expression of a creative spiritual dedication to the one true King. The contemporary interpreter must sensitively, imaginatively, and critically handle his materials. He must reconstruct the situation of those responsible for the form in which the materials have been transmitted. He must penetrate through such reconstruction to the original moment of divine-human encounter. Finally, he must stand in relation to the traditions which he is examining under the conditions of his own life. Each perspective in the interpretive process is fraught with peril. For it is possible to distort, misconstrue, and misapply the text or tradition at hand. But to renounce the critical task by taking refuge in the Scriptures as the inerrant Word of God is to confuse the voice of God with the voices of finite human spokesmen whose humanity filters, shapes, and unavoidably distorts that which it transmits.

Revelation, declares Buber, is not the disclosure of information about God but the human encounter with his presence. From the countless moment-gods of everyday experience, we form the image of a single Thou. The beliefs and traditions of our religious communities help us to shape our unified conception. But all of this accumulated knowledge of God must stand the test of his presence to a concrete *I*. Whenever the received contents of tradition come alive and address my consciousness, the revelatory process is continued. Although my situation and that of the biblical text before me are never completely identical, *"what happened once happens now and always, and the fact of its happening to us is a guarantee of its having happened."* Until I have responded to the direct, personal voice of revelation addressed to my own life, I cannot appreciate the record of revelatory experiences in the Bible. We must be careful not to distort Buber's approach. Unlike the typical use of the Scriptures in American religion which transforms isolated passages into moral exhortations and personal messages to the reader from the Spirit, Buber's dialogic criticism demands both a restoration of the text to divine-human encounter from which it has sprung and the imaginative application of the lessons of the past to the partly similar yet always dissimilar circumstances of the present.

Buber's attempt to balance historico-critical and existential approaches to the Scriptures is typical of his cautious reverence for tradition. The common humanity of all men suggests that the insights gained by any one man in the depths of his distinct situation are not wholly irrelevant to the quandaries of another. Although the Scriptures are not a handbook dropped from heaven for the solution of human dilemmas, the recorded struggles of patriarchs, prophets, and sages with (as well as *against*) the call of God illuminate our own confrontation with the divine. Buber contended that nothing could be more harmful to mankind than the loss of the collective lessons which religious traditions scrupulously preserve and passionately transmit.

But, as we have seen, Buber was dead set against the kind of spirituality and reverence for heritage which divert men from their everyday responsibilities in order to seek God. Although such religion offers us self-fulfillment in return for the sacrifice of our normal humanity, it removes us from the only place in which God can be met. Life with God apart from life with men is spiritual masturbation. Buber is not rejecting the value of solitude and prayer, but pointing to the fact that their significance resides in the end to which they are directed. Critical reflection and inner renewal are essential to the process of personal maturation. For only an established self can enter into *I-You* relation. But if the development of the *I* is the purpose of such meditative moments, the self-sufficiency of the *I* hardens and the capacity for authentic personal development diminishes. This kind of spirituality deludes a man into seeking inner self-satisfaction instead of legitimate spiritual life. Since it is much more convenient to deal with religion than with God, religious routine and spiritual discipline replace the divine summons to the tensions and perils of interpersonal responsibilities.

True religion is the whole life of real persons and real communities of persons in the actual world. False religion directs man to perform special acts, at special times, in special places, in order to establish beneficial dealings with a world above or beyond. But even such religiosity may become paths to partnership with God. For through prayer and devotional exercises, the spirit of relation may seize a man without warning and force him against his will back to the world of the everyday. When spiritual seclusion sensitizes us to the forgotten responsibilities, to the ignored *You* in our life, then it is a vital part of our education as men.

Although God cannot be found apart from the world of men, involvement is no guarantee of godliness. Only an *I* can respond to a *You*. Running about seeking *I-Thou* encounters, forcing oneself upon others, is not authentic relation. The solitude which sifts through impression, memories, emotional responses, and thoughts in search of one's true self is an essential stage in coming to maturity. The hours spent in attending to the inner voices of conscience, reason, and faith are not the goal of religion, but there is no true religion (or true humanity) without them. *No spirituality is authentic which is incapable of responding to the fervent supplication: "Teach us to pray."*

But when the religious aspect of life separates itself from the everyday and becomes another activity alongside others, it loses its vital force which humanizes all of a man's concerns and involvements. The Eternal Thou whom we can never express but only address becomes a dogmatic formula. The living encounter of a man with the distinctive potentialities which lure him to fulfillment is replaced by the affirmation of creeds, doctrines, and maxims. God the *possessor,* the Lord and giver of life, becomes God the theological and per-sonal *possession.* The moment-by-moment response to the unfathomable presence calling us to hallow the everyday is transformed into the enjoyment of the divine in prescribed acts which of themselves produce his presence. The ever beckoning *You* who hides his face from us, disclosing only the signs of his presence, is supplanted by the God of the philosophers and theologians who serves the functions for which men require him. Instead of *response* to *Thou,* we offer *reliance* upon God. We believe in what we need—God the first cause who guarantees the rationality of our senseless existence, God the cosmic traffic cop who enforces the moral platitudes of the status quo, God the enormous mother who loves us despite ourselves, God the infinite mesmerist who shoots us full of positive suggestions. Such gods are little more than the projection of our psychic needs, and faith in them is nothing but an often repeated "I hope so." To worship such a God is to practice magic.

Buber recognizes that a conception of God must be both intelligible and mysterious. If it is not intelligible, it is not a conception. If it is not mysterious, it cannot be a conception of God. There is no such thing as knowledge of God as he is in himself. When we speak about God we refer to our relation to him. Since we have no other language than that which we use to communicate with one another regarding the mundane, this language must be pressed into service when we refer to the Eternal Thou. However, all talk about God will be logically queer. For we must employ our ordinary vocabulary and terminology in such a way that we underline the extraordinary nature of that to which we refer. We must speak metaphorically or symbolically.

Our actual encounter with the divine as the giver of the signs in all *I-You* relations is the basis for speaking about God at all. If there were no such dimension of our experience, we would be spared the tensions of religious language. But the reality of such encounters and our need to explore their implications in the communal life which they produce, impel us to interpret the character of the Eternal Thou. At the same time, the translation of encounter into language must be governed by the recognition of the insufficiency of all such efforts. For even the most exalted designations refer not to God but to our relation to him. We refer to God as the "eternal" Thou because he is always *You* and never anything but *You* to us. We call him "absolute" because his summons is unconditionally binding upon the consciousness of the one addressed. Whenever we attempt to represent him, we are doomed to fail. Nevertheless, at any moment we may lay aside all images and conceptions, and address the one enduring and unavoidable *You* who addresses us through the finite *You* at hand.

A man cannot be responsible to a theological formula but only to a *You.* Buber insists that even the pronoun "he" is a metaphor when spoken of God. It tells us more about the imagination and value structure of the speaker than it does about its alleged object. Since God is not an object, the less we *speak of* and the more we *speak to* the Eternal Thou, the better. For to speak *of* God is to reduce him to a thing which we can know, understand, use, and manipulate to our purposes. But to speak *to* God is to turn with one's whole being to the task of building the theocentric community of men.

Since it is partnership to which God calls us, Buber rejects those religious emphases which weaken man's ability to take up his share in the work of reconciliation. He reacts sharply to doctrines which direct our attention away from the hallowing of the everyday. For example, religious apocalypticism, the expectation of the divine victory over the forces of evil in the events of the Last Days, is opposed by Buber on the ground that it weakens the will of man to shoulder his own obligations for the world situation. Likewise, hope in life after death must not be allowed to become a central religious doctrine lest it drain off the passion of man's commitment to the here and now.

The issue of the extent of man's responsibility for the redemption of the world ultimately separates Judaism from Christianity. Since Buber believed that God manifests himself in countless forms—all of which point to the unity of the single transcendent Thou—he was willing to recognize the religious integrity of Christianity. However, he maintained that Christianity seriously misunderstood the concrete situation of the world and the duty of man in the face of this situation. According to Buber, the Church is grounded on the assumption that the Messiah has already come and that redemption has been accomplished. But as a Jew, Buber experienced the world's lack of redemption repeatedly in the awful sufferings and endless struggles of Jewish existence throughout his nearly ninety years.

Of course, the Church is not unaware of the tension between the appearance of the redeemer and the continued nonredeemedness of the world. The first coming of the Christ is seen as an anticipation of the glory which is to follow at the end of time. Similarly, the lives of redeemed men within the Church are indications of the full restoration of all to God at the coming of his Kingdom.

For Buber revelation is not a content but an encounter. Something happens to me which leaves me other than what I was before. I do not know something new. I have become something new, become someone. Revelation occurs when a powerful presence invades my life and transforms it. My life is no easier than it was before. If anything, it is vastly more complex, for it now bears meaning which it never previously possessed. I find myself burdened with significance and also responsible to work out all that such meaningfulness implies in the activities and encounters of my everyday life.

Revelation may happen anywhere, at any time, under any circumstances. It gives a meaning to my life which I can prove true only in the uniqueness of my life. When I reflect upon the revelatory meeting and attempt to rationalize the experience so that it can be repeated at desired times, or when I turn my attention from the duties of this newness of life to speculation about the object of the transforming experience, then the spontaneity of meeting becomes a discipline or a ritual, and the revealing presence becomes a dogma. Spirituality swells up and blocks the transforming power of the Spirit.

Every community, every society, every civilization, and every religion is based on an original moment of personal revelation. Revelation arises in the concrete circumstances of man's life and is therefore interpreted in terms of that situation. Each religion possesses a unique particularity, a suitability to the irreplaceable and unrepeatable circumstances in which it is born. But the doctrines, laws, norms of conduct, and liturgical practices by which the original revelation is made the basis of routine behavior by the group which has been grasped by revelation are not themselves revealed. As circumstances change, the religious cultus must change as well. Teachings which are relevant to one historic period must be reconceptualized in terms of the next. Laws which bind man to man in community during the external circumstances of one age must be recast under the impact of new situations. Of course, contemporaneity cannot be an end in itself. The notion that the task of religion is nothing other than conformity to the needs of the present is just as much a distortion as the attempt to impose past solutions on current problems. Religion is the transformation of man and his world in response to the divine summons. When religion loses its living Center, its standing in the revelatory situation, it no longer serves either the traditions of the past or the needs of the present.

The test of a religion is not the degree of its theological development or the beauty of its worship or the intensity of its devotional life, but the sensitivity of its adherents to the world of the everyday. According to Buber, the religious man is the one who knows how to talk *to* God even if he does not understand how to talk *about* God. The meeting with the divine Center of my life sensitizes me. My response to other persons becomes my major religious responsibility. In every concrete situation I must seek the greater self-realization of those with whom I am inextricably involved or risk the loss of my own self-realization.

But if the welfare of my neighbor is my responsibility, how can I possibly know of what my neighbor's good consists? Am I at the mercy of my feelings and instincts? Am I not as likely to meddle as to assist, to interfere as to confirm? It must be admitted that I can never be certain that my action is in the best interest of another. But at least I act. *I-You* sensitivity predisposes me to act and forbids my indifference. It does not give me general rules or maxims to govern my response. This is not to say that there is no source of prescriptions, but *I-You* openness is not the source.

In any society there is a group of basic ethical prescriptions. These are in fact descriptions of the features necessary for the continued existence of that society, the *sine qua non* of that form of communal life. The basic maxims concern the rights and responsibilities of the individual with regard to the group as well as the obligations of the group to secure his person, family, and property. The Ten Commandments may be regarded as a paradigm of such prescriptions. However, we must bear in mind that the universality of this particular code consists in the subjects which it concerns and not in the manner in which it treats them. There are many viable ways of regulating cultic practice, the use of force, the spoken word, family relations, sexual conduct, and personal property. But unless they are governed in some manner by the promulgation, application, and enforcement of rules, no human life is possible.

A society values those actions which most harmonize with its preservation, and condemns those which necessitate changes in its mode of existence. Change comes, but ordinarily only as the peripheral, nonessential modifications pile up. As long as the changes are assimilated into a sophisticated social image, as long as the desire for security and continuity prevents the fatal question about inconsistency from being asked, the process continues. As a matter of strategy, it is often wise to let it continue.

The religious man has little or no choice as to the kind of society in which he lives, but he can affirm or deny that society, detail by detail, law by law, maxim by maxim. When his sensitivity to the human potential of others requires it, he must deny some aspects of the present social and legal structure, perhaps much or all of the structure, and accept the social consequences. My personal encounter with God in the midst of the present situation may lead me to deny or affirm the prescription of society on some matter in general. For I may come to see that a given law or institution cannot but interfere with or enhance human potential. But all the while my ethical sensitivities are grounded not in principles but in concrete instances, not in rules but in my response to persons. This does not mean that my feelings permit me to transcend the rules. Law is the collective experience of a society's attempt to protect and maintain both its continuity and the welfare of its citizens. Within concrete instances, decision is guided by maxims, accepted norms of conduct, and religious moralities. Responsible decision is always in terms of such prescriptions even when it takes the form of opposition to rules.

It may appear that religion (in the narrower sense of the term, i.e., ecclesiastically sanctioned creeds and laws of conduct) makes no difference to the content of morality, but only to the attitude toward that content. In large measure, this is true. For society rather than religion is the source of ethical prescriptions. However, society is not a single voice but a mass meeting which hearkens to certain strong voices possessing the power to be heard above the general din. Religious institutions, by virtue of the solemnity of the issues with which they concern themselves (and due to the residual sentimentality which most Americans feel for the churches and synagogues which they have neglected since childhood), speak with inherent volume if not clarity. No degree of hypocrisy, irrelevance, or triviality can diminish this power. Thus, when the churches falter—as Catholicism has on the meaning of marriage and sexuality, as Judaism has on the extent of morality and responsibility, as Protestantism has in the matter of social justice—their sins are known by all, touch and influence all. When, on the other hand, the churches turn—as the Roman Catholic Church has on the legitimacy of other religions and the need for internal reform, as the Protestant churches have in increasing number on the right of selective conscientious objection, as Jews are beginning to turn to the recognition of the need for a variety of manifestations of religious experience within a family of faith and tradition—their transformation is a matter of concern to that entire society, churched and unchurched.

There are basic issues at stake in America today—the dignity of the human person, the value of the family, the meaning of social justice, the creative possibilities of peace, the function of the arts, the uses and limits of coercive power, the significance of responsible citizenship. Institutional religion is but one of several major voices offering guidance in these matters. Yet in many respects it is the most sensitive to the human situation—as those who once despaired at the indifference of the churches have come to acknowledge. For instance, the Rev. Andrew Young, Executive Secretary of the Southern Christian Leadership Conference, tells of leaving his former post with the National Council of Churches filled with frustration over the slow pace of Protestant commitment to the realization of racial equality. But, as he soon discovered, the bovinity of the churches was positively exhilarating compared to the complete intransigence of the American labor unions, realtors and, above all, the utter stupor of federal, state, and local lawmakers.

Despite their propensity for confusing godliness with the status quo, the churches have shown a greater willingness to harbor and encourage dissent, to protect the socially rejected such as the homosexual, and to defend the often self-obscured humanity of black nationalists, political malcontents, social dropouts, and artistic innovators than any other segment of our society. This ability to suffer fools gladly and to win sympathy for them reveals a power for more basic transformations of individual and social life which has only been slightly tapped.

In Buber's view, the instititutions are both the greatest obstacle to and the *sine qua non* for the actualization of true humanity. It is *in, through, and despite* the self-interest of the present ecclesiastical structures; *in, through, and despite* the factionalism of the suburban edifice explosion (no subdivision is complete without three competing Lutheran churches); *in, through, and despite* bake sales, bingo, sewing circles, and junior cherub choirs; *in, through, and despite* the follies, foibles, and frustrations of institutional religion that the spirit of God produces a remarkable number of authentic, concerned, responsible, and responsive men and women. The world may be where the action is, but it is, in large measure, *in, through, and despite* the institutions that men and women willing and able to struggle for the redemption of the world are recruited. It would appear that largely *despite* themselves, the churches and synagogues may be doing something right!

IV

Partnership in Suffering

If God is loving and all-powerful, why does he tolerate evil? If suffering is punishment for sin, why is it that the righteous are afflicted while the unrighteous prosper? If the Jews are in some special sense the people of God, why has He been blind to their anguish and sorrow during the long diaspora? If there is a God at all, why did he allow six million Jews—innocent men, women, and children—to be exterminated like insects? The problem of evil is not a mere academic exercise, but a cry of despair in the face of the inhumanity, barbarism, cruelty, injustice, and meaninglessness of man's existence. It's a fine world we live in. Have we not all been Jobs during the past few years? Young lives have been consumed in senseless wars which have destroyed a thousand times what they have gained. Men are called away from farms, homes, families, and forges so that their National Guard units can preserve our cities from riot and insurrection. Poisoned air and polluted water shorten the lives of millions. The good and the kind are cut off in the prime of life. Men of peace and apostles of the American dream are slain by insignificant nothings. Is there sense, or meaning, or God in any of this?

The Bible offers two contradictory solutions to the problem of evil: an official account and an almost suppressed minority opinion. According to the pious editors responsible for the redaction and transmission of the Hebrew Scriptures, history is governed by a strict pattern. The book of Judges is a rather extended illustration of the "cyclical view of history" which controls the selection and arrangement of materials in the Old Testament. Stage I of the cycle finds the children of Israel secure in their land. But peace and plenty turn their hearts from God and their contractual responsibilities to worship and serve him. Stage II of the cycle is the abandonment of the Israelites to conquerors who enslave and abuse them. Stage III is characterized by a turning to God in humble repentance and supplication. Penitence produces Stage IV, the sending by God of a deliverer who leads the people to victory over oppression. Stage V finds them secure in their land. But peace and plenty turn their hearts from God . . . and so on.

This view really came into its own at the time of the return from the Babylonian exile. Not only did the cyclical view make sense of the destruction of the kingdoms of Israel and Judah, but it provided a lesson for the future. The acceptance of the Torah, or Law of Moses, as the charter of corporate life and handbook for everyday behavior was based on this pious interpretation of the past. Furthermore, the accumulated traditions, writings, and remembrances of previous national life were rewritten, edited, and transformed in order to underwrite this view of history.

The cyclical view regards suffering as compensation for disobedience to the divine will. If man withholds his faithfulness to God, then the divine employer will instigate a lockout in response. If the rebel learns his lesson, the security-in-exchange-for-devotion relationship will be restored. If not, the consequences are on the striker's head. Or, to employ a more biblical simile: The nation Israel is a well-loved but adulterous wife. If struck regularly, she may come to her senses and return to her ever patient and forgiving spouse—an opinion which is based on an extremely naïve conception of the female psyche. The infidelity continues and so do the beatings. If Israel is fortunate, she will develop a distaste for unfaithfulness before the divine husband murders her with love.

Consonant with the cyclical view is the notion of individual freedom. God allows man to choose to obey of his own free will. Therefore, God must offer real alternatives, evil as well as good. In their created state, all things were good. But the continuous disobedience of man has got the world into its present rotten shape. Mismanagement rather than inferior materials account for the disharmonies and imbalances in nature and human affairs. Pain and suffering are meant to be remedial. The pig sties encourage the Prodigal to return to the father. But what of the apparent surplus of unproductive and counterproductive suffering such as the daily death by malnutrition of thousands of innocent children, the destitution and degradation of life in America's slums, the ignominious and unrecorded deaths of the hundred million voiceless victims of totalitarian regimes during the past half century. What purposes are served by mental retardation, cancer, genocide, and mass starvation? Christian advocates of the cyclical view tell us that such things teach us compassion. But does not the death of one child serve this purpose as well as the extermination of millions? What kind of man can worship and love the God who uses sorrow, death, and horror to achieve such small gains?

This very question is the point of departure of the subdominant stream of biblical theodicy. Even in its present censored form the book of Job presents a vastly different account from that offered by the pious redactors. The faith of Job insists that there is no spiritual "boom-bust" cycle, no balancing of the books by a divine accountant. Jobian realism acknowledges that Cosa Nostra leadership dwells secure in River Forest, Illinois, fully protected by the forces of law and order. In the world of living men, where the choice is between inefficient honesty and efficient corruption, the latter will win the fond embrace of even the most upstanding. Not only does evil triumph over good; it shows a far greater capacity for enjoying itself as well.

Job trusts God despite the contradiction of his faith by everyday experience. According to Buber, "he experiences and expresses without restraint the apparent godlessness of the course of the world and reproaches God with it, without however diminishing his trust in Him. . . ." After Auschwitz, Bergen-Belsen, and Buchenwald; after the murder of John and Robert Kennedy, Malcolm X, and Martin Luther King, Jr.; after the birth of pitifully deformed thalidomide babies; after the destruction by napalm and terrorism, American materialism and inner corruption, of genuine Vietnamese nationalism—after all of the images of the victory of inhumanity, bigotry, cruelty, and injustice have flooded our brains and soiled our souls—after the death of our childhood faith in the God who rewards righteousness and punishes sin—can we still believe? As Buber asks, "Dare we recommend to the survivors of Oswiecim, the Job of the gas chambers: 'Call to Him, for He is kind, for His mercy endurest forever'?"

According to Buber, the only basis for affirming the meaningfulness of life in the face of the insurmountable evils of human existence is the recognition that man's sufferings are also the sufferings of God, that man's struggle to realize good despite all that opposes him is at the same time God's ongoing creation of order out of primal chaos. The redemptive process through which the harmony and reunification are achieved is a divine-human undertaking, a partnership which exposes both man and God to opposition, defeat, and pain. Unless God himself participates in the heartaches and sorrows of man's earthly state, then all striving is in vain.

Contrary to our casual assumption, notes Buber, the creation story of Genesis does not describe a creation out of nothing but a struggle by the divine spirit to impose order and meaning upon the chaotic and meaningless. The formless void is much more than a mere empty null. For it contains all the possibilities, meanings, and values of reality. These building materials of being await the directing power of spirit in order that they may be formed, shaped, and utilized. The transformation of the confused and disarticulated cascade of potentialities into a creation, a world, a cosmos under the guidance of the divine personality establishes actuality and goodness in the place of possibility and chaos.

Like the cosmogonic myths of many ancient peoples, the creation accounts of Genesis mirror the process by which human personality arises out of the chaos of desires, urges, sensations, dreams, needs, and possibilities. In the period which generally coincides with puberty, the incipient human person becomes aware of the category of possibility, the realization that one's essence is not a fixed form which is given but a potentiality which can be created in a multitude of ways. The emerging personality is overwhelmed by a plentitude of possibility which confuses, bewilders, and terrifies. The swirling chaos of potential directions, aims, and purposes threatens to dissolve the tenuous hold of the self upon itself. The self can grab hold of any object which floats past the vortex that carries it, and cling to it in desperation. In this way, an identity is maintained by a holding to an ideal, a belief, a platitude, a satisfaction, etc. The swirling currents of possibilities continue, but all potentials save one are ignored. Another course is to yield to an inner voice which directs the emerging person to "set about the audacious work of self-unification." The centered self binds itself not to one possibility but, rather, to a direction which harmonizes and unites all possibilities.

Good is that which man does with the wholeness of his being; evil that which concerns only a part or segment of his total experience. Goodness is not achieved by the overcoming or suppression of some possibilities by others as the dualistic spirituality of Western religions assumes. It is not the denial of given impulses, talents, and proclivities which enables a man to attain the goodness of his distinct selfhood. Rather, it is the direction of one's whole being which is decisive. Nothing is good or evil in itself but good or evil only with respect to the purpose and intention of the self.

Rabbinic theology speaks of conflicting human *yetzerim* or impulses: *ha-yetzer ha-ra* (the evil impulse) and *ha-yetzer-ha-tov* (the good impulse). Were it not for the acquisitive, erotic *yetzer-ha-ra,* a man would never build a home, take a wife, beget children, or engage in business. Thus, even the so-called "evil impulse" may become the instrument of good, and any false spirituality which demands the repression of man's vital instincts counsels the destruction of man's humanity. However, when the *yetzer-ha-ra* remains without direction or purpose, it becomes the source of all the griefs which flesh is heir to—war, inhumanity, injustice, exploitation, and cruelty. According to Buber, it is man's task not to extirpate his inclination toward evil but to direct it to the actualization of good.

The selection of the single direction which unites the scattered forces of the self is not a once-and-for-all decision. Again and again, the centered self is overpowered by the miasma of new possibilities. The emerging personality is torn asunder almost as quickly as it finds definite and concrete form. The torrent of experience which it attempts to encompass refuses to be assimilated and tears the self to shreds. If it is not dispersed beyond recall, the self repeatedly attempts reunification. As Buber relates, the crystallization of a formed and stable self is attained through venture, risk, and suffering.

Every time a man gives himself wholly and unconditionally to a single direction, he fails. But such a setback gains for him an inkling of the one true direction. Through this "cruelly hazardous enterprise," he becomes the unique and whole person that only he can become. According to Buber, conscience is the voice which calls the developing self to fulfill the unique and never-to-be-repeated potentialities of its being. Coming to maturity is the coming to be of one's distinctive personality. It is the acceptance of the awesome and terrible responsibility of actualizing one's singularity. Very few individuals are willing or capable of making this dangerous response. There is a trace of autism in us all—a willingness to forgo the tensions and sorrows of becoming independent and unique persons. Nothing is more debilitating than the false humility of well-brought-up young people who allow their creative life's blood to drain away as evidence of their harmlessness to the status quo. As charming as they may seem, their sacrifices are a thousand times more evil than the exasperating self-assurance and cocky self-righteousness of those youthful malcontents who belittle and deride our bourgeois values and goals.

Guilt is the state of remaining with oneself, of refusing to venture out of the security of self-isolation. It grows out of the fear of being hurt, the terror of being used, the memory of past mistakes. It is the refusal to accept the responsibility for one's own life and the corresponding deafness to the call to respond to any other self. Finally, guilt is the willingness to drift rather than to decide upon direction. And it is from this lack of direction that all evils arise.

Buber declares that good is direction and all that follows from direction. Evil is a surrender to the momentary and the available, the instantaneous response to whatever presents itself. It shatters the unity of the self into a thousand conflicting and contradictory impulses, no two of which can occupy the attention of the individual at the same time. Thus the life of man is fractured into compartments, departments, concerns, urges, feelings, and needs. The acceptance of any one is the rejection of all others. In this way the false dichotomies which govern contemporary life and thought were born, i.e., subjectivity versus objectivity, rational versus emotional, impersonal versus personal, the hard facts versus human values, utility versus beauty, individual rights versus social responsibility. The result is the self-crucifixion of contemporary man—the youthful commitment to a stance or role followed by a lifetime of regret that the alternatives have been repressed. The intellectual sadly acknowledges that he is dead from the neck down. Disillusioned lovers rue the surrender of mind and the will to physical passion. Conscientious parents regret that Spock-Gesell-Ginott rather than an understanding heart governed their child-rearing duties.

Buber declares that evil cannot be done with the whole soul. It is a striking out at whatever is at hand—in his words "the grasping, seizing, devouring, compelling, seducing, exploiting, humiliating, torturing, and destroying of what offers itself." To a man without direction, there is neither right nor wrong. Adam and Eve partake of the forbidden fruit not because they have decided to do so but because they are sunk in a trancelike state of contemplation of possibilities which makes them oblivious to what they are doing. Cain kills Abel not because he has decided to murder but in order to confirm and intensify his basic indecision. In terms of our modern cinematic myths, Benjamin (the hero of *The Graduate*) does not seduce Mrs. Robinson. He ceases resisting because he has nothing better to do. His climactic snatching of Elaine Robinson from her wedding is not a reversal but a continuation of his indecision. He has made no decision. He has only yielded to the strongest of his impulses, the course of action which most appealed at the moment. Ten minutes after the events which end *The Graduate,* Ben will realize once more that his life is still aimless. Having a nuptially bedecked beauty and an empty wallet is a gas—for about half an hour.

Prolonged indecision constitutes a virtual decision for indecision. Indecision becomes a fixed course of action, a radical dedication to evil. As we have seen, man is the only creature which requires confirmation in order to actualize its nature. Since the plastic, changing, chaotic selfhood of the undirected individual offers nothing to be confirmed or rejected, it must affirm itself in order to survive the threat to its being posed by the nonconfirmation of others. The all-embracing image of what I should be is replaced by a determination to remain just as I am. Self-affirmation cuts the individual off from both the supportive power of external conformation and the possibility of correcting the one-sidedness of his self-image. For confirmation by others includes affirmation of a person's actual and potential value as well as the concerned rejection of anything which diminishes from his unrepeatable uniqueness.

At this stage, man becomes his own creator. Character hardens into a determined opposition by the individual to becoming the unique person he was intended to become. Isolated from the critical confirming interaction of man with man, the individual is cut off from the possibility of self-knowledge. The lives of such individuals become a series of carefully executed mimes and poses intended to give the appearance of developed personality. The awful fact, maintains Buber, is that God gives such "men" the power to persist in their rebellion. As the biblical references to the hardening of Pharaoh's heart illustrate, God's attempt to bring the man who opposes him to his senses persists only so long. The obdurately self-centered and self-determined individual reaches a point of no return, a moment in which he finds an inflexible determination to resist the summons to responsible selfhood. As Buber declares: ". . . sin is not an undertaking which man can break off when the situation becomes critical, but a process started by him, the control of which is withdrawn at a fixed moment." A perverted relationship between man and man, nation and nation, man or nation and God hardens into an inevitable destiny from which there is no possibility of return. The small misunderstandings, failures of judgment, moments of deafness, and unkept promises suddenly crystallize into a disaster of major proportions.

For Buber, freedom and responsibility are inseparable. Because man is fully free to accept or reject the way set before him by God, he is also fully responsible. Because he is fully responsible, he is truly free. Man's rights are his duties. It is only when we strip a man or a class of men of the power of responsible self-determination that we deprive them of freedom. The only right possessed by man in the political, academic, religious, social, or economic spheres of his existence is his complete responsibility. Responsibility without freedom is slavery. But freedom without obligation is abandonment to aimlessness, the very essence of evil. For each man and each nation, there is a direction or way to fulfillment. But as the narrative of Hebrew national existence makes clear, both persons and peoples may reject the direction which opens up before them and the life which attends their true path.

In terms of Buber's *I-Thou* philosophy, evil is refusal to

enter into relation, the determined puffing up of one's individuality and self-importance so that there is no need for confirmation of one's being by another. The self-made man is capable of dialogue only with his creator. His response to other persons is determined by the uses to which he can put them. Authentic love—the acceptance of the other as a definite responsibility and an unparalleled mutual opportunity—is replaced by the distorted affection which regards the other as a mirror for the perusal and enjoyment of one's own image. The other is no longer *my* partner in the actualization of *our* unique potentialities but a collection of desirable traits which complements and enhances the qualities which I already possess.

Direct, open dialogue fades into the exchanging of polite banter and the swapping of small benefits—"stroke for stroke" as Eric Berne suggests. The life of intimacy—the slow progress through blunders, misunderstandings, and sudden flashes of awareness; the shared sorrows and joys as well as the private regrets and delights; growth despite one's sins and being sinned against—this life becomes nothing more than a set of rigid techniques for the attainment of "meaningful (i.e., personally satisfying) interpersonal relations." The spontaneous, frightening, amazing, painful, renewing interplay of person with person gives way to the laborious re-creation of enjoyable experiences and inner states of satisfaction. The symbol of this attitude is the "marriage manual," a mechanic's handbook which offers paradigms of performance couched in appropriately obscure terminology so that lovers will know what they are up to. The intention, it would seem, is to foist such stringent norms upon those engaged in what is euphemistically and paradoxically termed "love-making" that they will discover that the whole business is a bother at best and a rather absurd form of behavior for adults to boot. If sexual pleasure requires subjugation to the remorseless, grimly serious hedonism of the *Playboy* philosophy, then perhaps novelist Mary McCarthy's belittling of the whole awkward, silly business is right on target. After all, the pursuit of happiness is not only tiresome and expensive but remarkably unrewarding. The attempt to legislate pleasure is as vain as the endeavor to legislate morality.

The activities which arise from the individual's quest for desirable states of experience—even if these activities are entirely altruistic—poison both the doer and the object. Thus, efforts at assisting the Negro which are prompted by white guilt-feelings are doomed from the outset. For they are rooted not in the desperation and suffering of the Negro but in the white need for inner repose. Unlike the motivating force of *true* guilt which acknowledges the failure to respond and which atones as best it can by accepting actual responsibility, the *felt* guilt of the self-professed liberal is insensitive to the concrete situation of black existence. Ultimately programs guided by any motive other than the concern of a person for a person are in vain.

Evil—in forms which range from insensitivity to the needs of one's neighbor to the deliberate destruction of human life and potential by the totally selfish individual—destroys both perpetrator and victim. According to Buber, the attempt at using evil to serve good leads to the dissolution and destruction of the good. But since Buber's use of the terms "good" and "evil" refers not to qualities which acts possess in themselves but to the direction or lack of direction of the doer, it must be asked whether the notion of "using evil" is not a contradiction in terms. Are not all the acts of a good man good? Clearly, a negative answer is demanded by experience and common sense. Evil is not only the *subjective* state of decisionlessness and the acts which arise from a firm commitment to a lack of decision. Evil is something quite objective, namely, the harming of any being with whom I stand in relation. If I in any way lessen or diminish another, then I detract from my own personal worth.

Buber recognizes that to live is to be guilty of inflicting pain and committing injustice. We cannot even breathe and eat without destroying life. In our social existence, the preservation of the community involves us in the withholding as well as the sharing of human rights. What really matters, Buber asserts, is that we are aware of our responsibility and determine exactly how much injustice is necessary to preserve the community. If we are to avoid even greater guilt than that which ordinarily accrues to our social existence, we must accept no more than the bare minimum of necessary evil.

Buber insists that precise limits must be set to the self-protection of society. This requires that the standards, norms, and guiding aims by which a society measures dangers to itself be continually re-examined. One need only recall the damage wrought by Senator Joseph McCarthy's witch-hunting to the reputations and careers of thousands of innocent Americans. Never was liberty so poorly defended. Buber acknowledges the legitimate need of the body politic to protect its existence even if it must resort to violence to do so. Likewise the individual must sometimes use force for the protection of his own life and the lives of his family.

The goal of peace should govern the actions of men and nations. However, peace without justice is not peace at all, but merely the sublimation of conflicts under the threat of punishment. True peace allows the fulfillment of diverse personalities and divergent groups. The imposition of the will of the majority upon individuals and groups which are too weak to resist situations detrimental to their progress is actually a state of war between majority and minority interests. Unless such injustice is resisted both in the heart of the individual and in the governing processes of the state, the possibility of true justice and peace will be obliterated. It is clear that both oppressor and oppressed are responsible for the termination of injustice. Those rare members of the privileged majority who are sensitive to the subtle and undeclared war against the non- and underprivileged must seek an end to the injustices which deprive both oppressor and victim of their humanity. The victim is responsible to transform passive suffering into creative resistance, if necessary using directed violence in his own defense. In both cases, the struggle against injustice in the world is a legitimate and necessary expression of the constant struggle between order and chaos through which individuality is transformed into personality.

However, certain paths are obvious transgressions of the limits of self-protection. Buber was an unflinching foe of capital punishment, wars of aggression, and chauvinism. For Buber, capital punishment is virtually an act of involuntary suicide, the destruction by the community of a portion of its own life. Although it is intended to deter men from criminal behavior, it drives them still more deeply into the personal confusion out of which evil arises. Finally, we may infer from Buber's writings an unspoken but implicit objection. Capital punishment assumes that evil cannot be redeemed, that the murderer is radically beyond the rehabilitating power of interpersonal dialogue. But, argues Buber, it is not enough to resist and conquer evil. The goal of the divine-human partnership is the transformation of evil into good, and the reconciliation of the divisions which set man against man, man against society, man against himself, and man against God. Thus, the repression of antisocial actions can never offer more than temporary protection.

Since violence drowns out the possibility of communication—the one path by which evil may be transformed into good—its use must be severely restricted. War represents the complete failure of human dialogue. To Buber the most grievous war of the several conflicts which raged during his lifetime was neither World War I which swept away once and for all the politics, class structure, morality, and religious certainties of European civilization, nor World War II which saw the systematic murder of six million of Buber's coreligionists. The conflict which broke his heart was the Arab-Israeli war for the control of Palestine. For these frequently renewed hostilities destroyed Buber's fervent hope for a genuine peace between Arab and Jew, the flowering of a nation in which diverse peoples could live together in concord and cooperation. Buber had dared to dream of a nation capable of transcending the narrow self-interests and expansive aspirations of all other countries. The partition of Palestine into separate Jewish and Arab states and the subsequent bloodshed not only shattered Buber's vision but further intensified the dangerous rifts between the world's powers.

Instead of surmounting the evils of previous national rivalries, Israel has exemplified them during her short history. Although her enemies have shown little desire in a lasting peace, Israel has consistently flaunted the forces of international law which have sought to breach the chasm between the brave young nation and her neighbors. Since the establishment of the United Nations, no country has been more frequently cited for violations of the peace. Buber feared that the only lesson which the Jewish people had learned from the holocaust was that sufficient force can silence any moral outcry. He was not reluctant to condemn "might makes right" tendencies of Israeli policy, particularly the abduction, trial, and execution of Adolf Eichmann.

A particularly striking illustration of the realism of Buber's concept of evil is provided by his evaluation of the guilt of the German nation. Buber is careful to distinguish varying degrees of complicity in the genocidal horrors of the Third Reich. First, he observes, there were those who knew what was happening in the death camps but who offered no opposition. Second, there was the great mass of Germans who knew about the mass murders and cremations only as vague rumors. These "average" Germans made no attempt to discover the truth behind the rumors for fear of having to face a guilt which could not be borne. Third, there were those who learned what was taking place and who refused to cooperate with the apparatus of genocide. Many in this group forfeited their lives or committed suicide rather than participate in the inhumanity of the Nazi regime. Finally, there were many thousands of Germans who played a direct role in the systematic murder of millions of Jews and other "subhumans."

In Buber's view, the last group so removed themselves from the human race by their monumental inhumanity that it is impossible to feel any genuinely human emotion toward them.

They are worthy neither of hatred nor of the overcoming of hatred. But Buber's reverence and love for those Germans who gave their lives in opposition to the implementation of the "final solution" made it impossible for him to condemn the mass of Germans. Buber insisted that the efficient inhumanity of some Germans must not be considered indicative of the "German character." As for those who had been indifferent to the fate of the Jews, Buber felt himself unable to condemn men for refusing to follow the path of martyrdom. On the other side of the ledger, Buber found among German youth who had come to adulthood in the postwar years a deeper awareness of the ongoing struggle for true humanity than among the young people of any nation—including his adopted homeland, Israel. As a "surviving arch-Jew" Buber was proud to accept both the Hanseatic Goethe Prize and the Peace Prize of the German Book Trade as symbols of his continued alliance with all Germans who have dedicated their lives and talents to the achievement of a lasting peace.

Although Buber's description of the culpability of the German nation recognizes varied degrees of responsibility, there can be no question that each and every German who was an adult during the National Socialist regime shares a basic guilt, i.e., the failure to respond to one's fellows. For, in the last analysis, evil is in its very essence the universal rejection by men of their actual responsibility for other human beings. The guilt of the Nazis differs more in degree than in kind from the day-by-day insensitivity to the potentialities and needs of those with whom we are involved. Evil arises when our apparent independence and self-sufficiency blind us to the actual interdependence of all men.

According to Buber, God invites *individuals* to become *persons* by entering into partnership with him in the redemption of the world. God calls on each man to renounce the self-deception of directionless, self-centered life. Each person is invited in the uniqueness of his being to direct his distinctive selfhood—his character, attainments, and abilities—to the reunification of the tragic divisions which desolate personal life, devastate interpersonal relations, and destroy the divine-human meeting. By "turning" *(teshubah),* says Buber, by forsaking the hardness which divides and separates human beings, man participates in the work of redemption.

The Christian conception of "repentance" represents an unfortunate psychologizing of the act of turning. Buber insists that the turning involves the whole man in the concreteness of his present existence. The act of turning is as little an inner psychic occurrence as is a man's birth or death. The turning has its primary effects not in the secret recesses of the soul but in the sphere of man's meeting with man. It is not what happens *within* but what occurs *between* which is decisive.

The turning restores a man to his original dialogic relation to God—but it by no means is concerned with or directed toward God. The relation of "the undivided human being to the undivided God" involves man with the fullness of his earthly existence. Just as God's creative activity embraces man's corporeality as well as his spiritual life, so the redemption to which he calls man encompasses the whole man—body, soul, and spirit. Man cannot fulfill the obligations of his partnership with God through a "religious" life but only by hallowing every area, sphere, and dimension of his existence. Buber argues that there is no final gulf between the sacred and the profane, the secular and the holy. The world of human experience is not divided into the sanctified and the unsanctified, but into the *holy* and the *not yet holy.* God calls man to serve him with all his powers, urges, drives, and desires without subtraction, repression, or sublimation. For only an undivided person can share with the undivided God in the restoration of all things to their true direction.

Buber's critics have accused him of advocating a "Jewish activism" which exalts man's power and disregards the need for divine grace. In reply, Buber declares that neither the power of redemption nor the call to partnership resides with man. All that man possesses is responsibility—his openness to the divine summons in every aspect of his concrete, everyday existence. The inclination to hear is man's; but the voice that speaks is not. As Buber maintains, there can be no reply without an appeal; no responsibility unless there is One to whom man is responsible. As each man responds to the drum which sounds for him alone, he participates in the redemption of his world. As a man directs his energies to the fulfillment of his distinct capabilities, he cooperates with the divine creator in the actualization of all potentialities.

In his never-ending dialogue with each man, God reveals not the mystery of his being, but the particularity of the life of his human partner. Revelation is neither information about God nor a prescribed set of norms for the regulation of conduct. It is the unpredictable, unforeseeable manifestation of one's true direction again and again in the course of life. The God who cannot be fathomed by human reason binds himself to man through mutual relationship. But man finds the tension, uncertainty, and astonishment of living encounter with God so unbearable that he places religion between himself and God. Through dogma, ritual, and rules, man establishes a bridge between his world and the presence of God—a bridge required not by a real gulf between creator and creature but, rather, by the desire for distance on the part of man.

But, Buber continues, the true God of the divine-human encounter decrees the death of all images of himself and all structures which seek to replace his menacing presence with routine behavior. The God to whom we pray, to whom we direct our worship, in whom we trust is but a figment of our imaginations. Contemporary man's proclamation of the death of God is not mistaken. Every attempt at fashioning a final conception of God, or a once-and-for-all institution which mediates his presence, or a universally valid set of moral prescriptions proves futile. Again and again, man's discomfort with the nakedness of divine-human meeting forces him to create such images. But no sooner is the new image installed than it disintegrates under the pressures of everyday life.

Buber advocates an audacious faith which clings to the

hidden speaker despite the destruction of all idols. "The images topple, but the voice is never silenced." Religion, in its despair at the contradictions and frustrations of daily existence, proclaims a salvation of the soul, an escape from the ambiguities and perils of human life. But true spirituality experiences *contradiction as theophany.* The world is seen by both the "religious" and the "spiritual" man divided into redeemed and unredeemed spheres. To the religious man, the present conflict suggests an eternal duality between good and evil which can be overcome only by rejecting one or the other. But, according to the spiritual man, God cannot permit half of reality to persist in its unredeemedness. The tragedies of human existence play their part in the ongoing redemption of reality. The pains and sufferings of life are not the opposite of redemption but the very arena in which it comes to triumph after its many setbacks.

To the man of faith, there is God in all this. As Buber boldly asserts, *man cannot know God but he can imitate him.* By entering into his life with all the active fullness of his created uniqueness, each man brings that portion of reality for which he is responsible to its consummation. Like the divine redeemer, the man of faith feels salvation happening *and* feels the unsaved world. The participation of such a man in the divine process of reconciliation exposes him to the highest joy as well as the most acute sorrow. In his own life, he anticipates and enjoys the coming of the all-embracing, all-fulfilling rule of God. But, at the same time, his share in redemption reveals the frustration of purpose and the resultant suffering and despair which attends man's personal and social existence. The unendurable pain which the man of faith experiences in the presence of the recurrent contradiction of the divine intention for mankind may be dealt with in two ways. The spiritual man may accept a creative cosuffering with God and bend his efforts to the redemption of the evil at hand. Or he may be so overcome with the painful contradiction of evil that he renounces any influence over the affairs of the state and society. The choice, then, is between *godliness* and *godlikeness,* between a religiosity which abandons the world to its unfathomable perversity and a partnership in the sufferings of the God who woos all things to a consummation and fulfillment which they persistently resist. In the end, each man must decide whether it is better to save the world by attending to that fragment under one's control, i.e., himself, or to refuse to climb the wall into personal fulfillment until the entire world of one's responsibilities and relationships has been exposed to the possibility of fulfillment.

V

The Future of Buber

Several factors have contributed to a general demise in the consideration and application of Buber. Ironically, these same factors indicate his real permanence and continuing importance. The relegation of Buber to the footnotes and archives of religious thought may be traced to one fundamental oversight on the part of his interpreters and disciples. All too often, we have approached Buber's dialogic philosophy in terms of our goals rather than his. For many of us, the central problem of contemporary existence is what Emil Durkheim terms *anomie*—the confusion and anxiety which result from the disintegration of established social and cultural ties. We tend to look to Buber for salvation from the repudiated, repressive, self-alienating social, cultural, and religious forms. But instead of promising us a new community arising from the ashes of the old, Buber attempts the annoying and perhaps impossible task of demonstrating the relevance of the ancient faith, to which he had committed his life and destiny, to the contemporary situation.

His central teachings, e.g., the dialogic essence of human personality, the inseparability of the divine-human encounter from the concrete responsibilities of man for man, relate his understanding of the meaning of Jewish life to the dilemmas of modern society. Buber pursued, and encourages us to pursue, a "method of correlation," a creative reinterpretation of our religious heritage under the impact of the real world of daily experience, and, further, an application of the essence of our religious tradition to those contemporary quandaries which remain insoluble from every other perspective. In a manner which parallels Tillich's Christian theology of correlation, Buber closes the gap between ancient faith and modern man through a critical, prophetic response to culture, i.e., man's self-understanding as expressed in the art, literature, law, social institutions, and political structures of the present. The constant re-evaluation of religion and culture in terms of one another produces basically theological solutions to' the human predicament, that is, answers which *apply to* (and which are not merely *derived from*) man's stumbling efforts to discover and actualize meaning in all spheres of his existence. In addition, Buber regards the contemporary situation as but one instance of the life of man as man. There are no cultural phenomena *sui generis.* In each period of his history, man has responded to certain basic dilemmas in ways which are highly diverse yet essentially similar. Thus, the undeniable power of the discoveries of contemporary man to illuminate his situation suggests that the present provides important tools for the exploitation of the past. The application of Judaism (or Christianity) to the present predicament is an absurd undertaking unless traditional faith is willing to expose itself to the critical scrutiny of contemporary culture. What comfort can biblical answers offer us in the age of Marx, Freud, Kafka, and Huxley if they have not been shaped and formed by the tensions of dialogue with this age?

Because we desperately need the results of Buber's lifelong wrestling with religious tradition and the modern world, we have seized his answers without duplicating his struggles. But unless we accept the scandalous Jewishness and painful modernity of Buber, we will vulgarize rather than appropriate his contributions. Buber the universal humanist and humanitarian—the Buber who appeals to us so strongly—is a trivial, poetic romantic. The starting point for both the interpretation and the re-creation of Buber's life is not, as we have inclined ourselves to think, his conversion from the quest for mystical union with God to the life of dialogue *but the struggle of a religious man with an unredeemed world.* The meaning of

Buber's conversion is the realization that the sacred and profane are inseparable. Each is incomplete without the other and attains its final consummation only at the very heart of the other. The failure to recognize the reciprocity of the religious and the secular has given birth to two errors: self-contained religiosity and self-sufficient secularism. The former regards the separation of the religious and the worldly as eternally unbridgeable. Instead of supplying the power to transform and enhance the secular, self-contained religiosity encourages the spirit to fall into spirituality and for religion to become an end in itself.

In reaction to the irrelevance, arrogance, and tyranny of self-contained religiosity, the equally mistaken secular theologies and one-world reductionisms have arisen. Secular theology has attempted to live on the compounded interest of traditional religion while denying the existence of any accumulated capital. Although such theology rightly emphasizes the secular as the proper area of religious concern, it ignores the locus of spiritual birth and renewal. As Buber recognized, the task of the spirit is the creative brooding over the face of the secular depths. But such creativity does not arise by spontaneous generation.

As tempting as it may be to enlist Buber in behalf of a secular theology, it is impossible. For the sphere of interpersonal relations and the mystic's quest for ecstatic union with the divine form a single, indivisible *Gestalt* like the familiar Chinese *Yin-Yang*. The mystic is called not to forsake his experience of a living God but to direct it to its true aim, the reconciliation of all things (and not merely the mystic's ego) to the divine creator and fulfiller. The religious man is not summoned to irreligion but to the difficult reinterpretation of religion under the impact of the real world of the everyday. It is one of the great tragedies of the twentieth century that the community of authentic yet contemporary Jews which Buber, Franz Rosenzweig, and others personally trained was destroyed in embryo by the agents of the "final solution." Until a generation of Jews fills out the implications of

Buber's suggestions, the viability of his world-oriented Judaism will remain untested.

While many of us have been striving to get out of the institutions which stifle our initiative and betray our ideals, Buber was struggling to get in. No doubt he was haunted by the image of Kierkegaard, the pathetic prophet who cut himself off from all human relationships in a vain endeavor to serve the God who cannot be met apart from the responsibilities of the everyday. As Buber insisted, God has hidden his hearing in the deafness of men. A word, deed, or life which is directed to Him without being directed to the concrete needs of men will never attain its goal. Likewise, the call of God to each man is partially transmitted and partially obscured by each human voice. Whatever the defects of traditional religions, they represent the most persistent attempt to hear and heed the divine summons. No matter how badly they distort the voice of the Spirit, it is *in, through, and despite* the community of faith that this voice is heard at all. If the inner voice of personal revelation remains unconfirmed within the community of those who have struggled not only to hear and respond to the divine call but to convey their burden to successive generations, we would do well to ask the true identity of the speaker.

If a man is to discover the meaning of his unique selfhood, he must start with the heritage of faith, disbelief, and doubt which has made him the particular man he is. No man can advance far along the path to self-understanding until he grapples with the inescapable question: What does it mean to be a Jew (or a Christian)? A re-examination of one's emerging personality in the light of the past so that the *cul-de-sacs* of the past may be avoided is one reason for returning to this question—but hardly the most important. Rather, the fight for one's place within Judaism or Christianity issues from a recognition of the essentially communal character of human personality as well as the awful realization of the propensities for self-delusion of stubborn individualism. If a man cannot find direction and fulfillment within the exclusive units of human development—friendship, marriage, family, and religious community—it is unlikely that he will achieve any greater success in the all-inclusive sphere of divine-human partnership.

Another difficulty in interpreting Buber results from his immersion in the concrete. Buber's writings fare badly in the hands of those devoid of experience, as for instance, the young. A work such as *I and Thou* builds upon fragments of lived sharing. It makes sense only to those who have experienced such concrete moments. When the neophyte ransacks Buber's thought for vicarious life the way he does a contemporary novel for vicarious sex, he is apt to be disappointed. The very concreteness of Buber's thought can make it seem vague and murky.

What other contemporary religious thinker could have written the following?

> A man caresses a woman, who lets herself be caressed. Then let us assume that he feels the contact from two sides—with the palm of his hand still, and also with the woman's skin. The twofold nature of the gesture, as one that takes place between two persons, thrills through the depth of enjoyment in his heart and stirs it. If he does not deafen his heart he will have—not to renounce the enjoyment—but to love. *(Between Man and Man,* New York, Macmillan, 1965. p. 96.)

Such writing may be *re-created* by personal participation but scarcely *understood* by generalization.

The concreteness of Buber's thought runs counter to much that currently passes for theologizing. Our younger theologians seem intent upon replacing experience with slogans, concealing rather than illuminating the actual. Aesthetic criteria—structure, style, and wit—count more than resonance with the real and everyday. Small wonder that vogue supplants vogue, that yesterday's radicals fade away like yesterday's top ten recordings, not because they are refuted but because we have heard them once too often.

The sole use of language which outstrips and overpowers Buber is profanity. The most enduring, concrete, forceful, and direct words in any language are its swear words. We hedge, protect, and defend the electric force of "four-letter" words from becoming tame and ignorable with a zeal which we devote to no other kind of language. The words which everybody knows but few utter in polite company re-create concrete animal functions with such clarity and directness that we are compelled to shudder. What theology sorely lacks is this very power of unambiguous communication. And such "profanity" is precisely what Buber brings to religious language. Until theology causes us to cringe, it merely conceals the real behind aphorisms, neatly turned phrases, and platitudes. The future of religion lies in its ability to proclaim that *"G-O-D" is a four-letter word* and not a euphemism which conceals the unpalatability of human existence.

The concreteness of Buber's thought gives his writing a bodily or tactile corporeality. His words become flesh and dwell among us. Buber observes that the Jew feels the world's lack of redemption "against his skin, he tastes it on his tongue, the burden of the unredeemed world lies on it." Similarly, Buber's writings establish a physical contact between writer and reader. He does more than touch our minds. His words press against us, stare into our eyes, and place a hand on our shoulders. The psychosomatic, holistic Jewishness of Buber's thought differs radically from the body-and-soul dualism of most religious discourse. A given theologian may annoy us; another confuse us; and yet another persuade us. But we scarcely feel physically oppressed by a presence which penetrates the written word. Religious writing and preaching seem to be dominated by a disdain for the physical-sensual aspects of human existence and by an overestimation of the intellectual. Perhaps our incipient theologians have been overtrained in philosophy, logic, and science and underexposed to literature and poetry. For no matter how airtight his arguments, or grandiose his structure, or timely his themes, *a religious thinker who is unable to speak to the psychosomatic wholeness of man, to the physical as well as the spiritual actuality of human life, is engaging in nothing more than academic exercises.*

An example of the manner in which we have turned away from Buber's concern for the concrete and actual and to the theoretical and academic is the area of interreligious dialogue. A fundamental lesson which emerges from Buber is that the dialogic philosophy is not a philosophy of dialogue. There is little in Buber about the structured presentations of serial monologues which pass for dialogue on today's ecumenical scene. Conversations between representatives of ecclesiastical organizations may accidentally become dialogue. But the official conferences of various kinds of Christians, or of Christians and Jews, or of the Judeo-Christian tradition with Eastern religions are in no sense examples of the concrete meeting of person with person advocated by Buber. Such conferences anticipate that communion grows out of dialogue. Actually, dialogue presupposes communion. Unless men are already united by a sense of mutual responsibility for an actual human need, conversation produces nothing but words. Whenever shared dilemmas draw men together in a community of concern, conversation manifests and achieves communion.

Thus, the talking about talking which characterizes so-called Jewish-Christian dialogue is misdirected. True dialogue is a continuous openness to God's offer of partnership, a sensitivity to the disparity between "is" and "ought to be." Wherever I share with another a sense of responsibility for a concrete instance of the denial of justice, the contradiction of humanity, or suppression of free creativity, we stand together in community and dialogue. It is to the unignorable issues of our times that we should direct our attention and efforts rather than to the pseudo-issue of "dialogue."

I have suggested that the factors which render Buber difficult to interpret and impossible to appropriate are themselves indications of the promise which he holds for the future of religious thought. For no matter how unsatisfactory we may find his personal solution, we are forced to return again and again to his central dilemma: At a time of rampant *anomie,* when all values rapidly become disvalues, when all stable forms of social and cultural life are disintegrating, when the

God of the Fathers is indeed dead—during such an age, what does it mean to be a Jew (or a Christian)? To those reluctant men and women who find themselves Jews or Christians against their wills, who experience the perverse grace which prevents them from refusing to be Jews and Christians, who find themselves bound to a God whom they steadfastly deny—to *us* the thought and example of Martin Buber will remain of utmost significance.

For he opens our eyes to the frightening possibilities of a lifetime of brutal, day-by-day struggle with God, man, and our own most private selves. He entices us not with euphemisms and well-turned phrases, but with a glimpse of the joys and sorrows of partnership with God. Without deluging us with ideology or smothering us in ideals, he fills our minds with images of the concrete, never-to-be-repeated potentialities of our lives, and, thereby, tempts us to forget the maxims and platitudes which shield us from responsible selfhood.

By becoming a *Thou* to all who will grapple with the concrete presence permeating his writings, by staring into our eyes and tugging at our lapels in a way duplicated by few writers, he points to a road and raises in each of us the hope that this way leads to justice, reconciliation, and wholeness. But is he an honest guide? Can we trust his directions? Was he able to attain his goal by following this path? And even if he did, is there any guarantee that others will succeed by going this way? Must we not declare his answers too simple, too seductive, too Buberian? Can it be denied that his analyses are one-sided, that his viewpoint is overly subjective, his style turgid and grandiloquent?

But if I may adopt the classical Jewish manner and answer these questions with a question—do not these very questions reveal the permanent, abiding significance of Buber? For as much as we may oppose and resist him, we are never quite able to let go of him. Within and between ourselves, in our discussions and disagreements, we struggle with Buber's issues and reinterpret Buber's answers—whether we are aware of it or not. We may choose to ignore him, we may even scorn his teachings, but in agonizing over the meaning of our humanity and the inexorable ties which bind humanity to deity, the dialogue continues and Martin Buber remains partner to us all.

Suggested Readings
in Martin Buber's Works

Chapter I. Martin Buber

A Believing Humanism: My Testament, 1902-1965.
Translated with an Introduction and Explanatory
Comments by Maurice Friedman. New York:
Simon and Schuster, 1968.

For the Sake of Heaven. New York: Atheneum. 1968.

Hasidism and Modern Man. New York: Harper Torchbooks, 1966.

Israel and the World: Essays in a Time of Crisis. New
York: Schocken Paperback, 1963.

On Judaism. New York: Schocken Books, 1967.

The Origin and Meaning of Hasidism. New York:
Harper Torchbooks, 1966.

*Tales of the Hasidim. The Early Masters and the Later
Masters* (two volumes). New York: Schocken
Paperback, 1961.

Chapter II. The Meaning of Personal Existence

Between Man and Man. New York: The Macmillan
Company, 1965 (paperback).

I and Thou. New York: Charles Scribner's Sons, 1960
(paperback).

The Knowledge of Man. Edited with an Introduction by
Maurice Friedman. New York: Harper Torchbooks, 1966.

Pointing the Way. Edited with an Introduction by
Maurice Friedman. New York: Harper Torchbooks, 1963.

Chapter III. The Spirit and the Forms

Eclipse of God: Studies in the Relation Between Religion and Philosophy. New York: Harper Torchbooks, 1957.

The Kingship of God. New York: Harper and Row, 1966.

Moses: The Revelation and the Covenant. New York: Harper Torchbooks, 1958.

The Prophetic Faith. New York: The Macmillan Company, 1949 (paperback).

Two Types of Faith. New York: The Macmillan Company, 1951 (paperback).

Chapter IV. Partnership in Suffering

For the Sake of Heaven.
On Judaism.
Good and Evil: Two Interpretations. New York: Charles Scribner's Sons, 1953.

For a full bibliography of Buber's writings, see Paul Arthur Schilpp and Maurice Friedman, editors, *The Philosophy of Martin Buber,* in *The Library of Living Philosophers* (LaSalle, Ill.: The Open Court Publishing Company, 1967). For a bibliography of books and essays by and about Buber through 1960, see Maurice Friedman, *Martin Buber: The Life of Dialogue* (New York: Harper Torchbooks, 1960).

A fine of TEN CENTS
each day the book is

RETURNED